Dear Football Moms

YOUTH FOOTBALL TO 12TH GRADE

DEAR Football MOMS!

A No-Nonsense
Guide to College
Football
Recruitment
& Eligibility

ALVIANNE BRULE'

SPORTS HEART PUBLISHING, LLC
NEW ORLEANS, LA

Dear Football Moms: A No-Nonsense Guide to College Recruitment & Eligibility — 1st Edition

ISBN-13: 978-0-692-04237-3

Published in the United States by Sports Heart Publishing, New Orleans, LA.

Author websites: alviannebrule.com, TheVIIITH.com

Connect at info@dearfootballmoms.com.

Book edited by Nakia J.S. Thomas of Fresh Editors & Writers.

Book designed by Art of Fresh Creative.

This book is dedicated to my mom who raised me as a single woman and helped me become the woman that I am today. I also dedicate this book to single mothers who are raising student-athletes alone and to all football moms who are committed to educating themselves and ensuring their sons realize and reach their full potential.

You are superwomen. I salute you!

CONTENTS

God is within her, she will not fall;
God will help her at break of day.
Psalms 46: 5 (NIV)

NEWS FLASH

MOST PARENTS OF student-athletes assume that if their child is talented enough, they'll automatically receive an athletic scholarship. Unfortunately, this isn't the case. In reality, athletic ability alone isn't enough. To attend college on a scholarship, the athlete must first qualify academically. If the athlete fails to qualify, he will typically attend a junior college, and after graduating, he will try to get re-recruited to play at a higher level.

The truth is that being accepted to play Division 1 college sports is a lofty, almost unreachable goal. So often, athletes will have to settle for Division 2 or Division 3 schools just to obtain a small scholarship. In this case, they or their parent(s) will take out a loan to pay for the remaining tuition costs. With nearly 70 percent of student-athletes coming from single-mother homes, this is usually not a feasible option. To make matters more difficult, most scholarships don't apply across all four years of college. Instead, the scholarships must be renewed yearly.

Once the athlete *is* in college, he must achieve and maintain a required GPA. If not, he will be ineligible to play due to poor academic performance and risk getting kicked out of the university. No matter how much we fight it or shy away from it, academics play a key role in student-athletes moving to the next level. Academics are the foundation — the "ticket," as I like to call it — for playing on the next level. Throughout this book, I hope to bridge the gap between academics and athletics and to help parents get more involved.

Parents often have false expectations of schools, coaches and counselors; they believe that these leaders, not themselves, are responsible to get their children into a Division 1 college with a full scholarship. However, parents of student-athletes must take responsibility for their children and educate themselves on the process their child will have to go through to play sports at the next level.

Hopefully, this book will be a key to unlock understanding and create dialogues, leading us to do better by our student-athletes and put them on a path to success. We need to start early (8th Grade) because the criteria keeps getting stricter, not easier. The longer a parent waits to learn, the more he or she puts their child at risk of ineligibility. This is something we need to educate ourselves on *now*.

This book is meant to specifically empower mothers. (Though fathers and student-athletes should read it, too.) As women, we are taught implicitly that we don't belong in the world of sports and that we lack understanding — so, in the past, we've taken the back seat.

Perhaps you don't know anything about football. That's fine. Learn the business of the industry. With knowledge, we can better promote change in our student-athletes' lives, including their academics, eligibility, and life after football. Leave the minutes of the game to the coach and we can handle life after football and this eligibility thing. I encourage you to learn it, master it, and make sure your student-athlete does what's necessary to be successful, both on and off the field.

Young athletes enter the foreign and strange world of collegiate and professional sports, in which they must learn to potentially navigate expensive contracts and hundreds of other psychological stressors. They shouldn't have to face these challenges alone and unprepared.

If we can successfully instill a mindset in our student-athletes that *sports are temporary* — ensure their identities aren't found in their athletic statuses alone — we can prove there are other rewarding paths worth following, in addition to sports. I hope this book creates dialogue amongst parents (especially single mothers) and their student-athletes, so we can change the narrative about what happens to them as they navigate the sports industry and reach for their goals.

INTRODUCTION

The Story Behind My "Why"

"I KNOW A YOUNG man who's being recruited to college and it's tearing our family to shreds," said a woman who'd called into the local radio station to reach me during an interview.

"They're not talking," she went on. "Can you come and talk to him and his parents and see if you can help our family out?"

At the time, I was running a sports management and marketing firm representing multiple NFL players off the field, handling all aspects of their philanthropy efforts, football camps, branding, relocation affairs and nearly every matter that their agents didn't want to deal with. I was mainly focused on helping players build a positive image in their communities and implementing programs and events for youth.

The woman over the radio knew what type of work I was invested in, but what she didn't know was that she was asking me to step out of my element. NFL players — from recruitment to retirement, with all the ups and downs — I knew all too well, but I had absolutely no concept of what was going on with high school student-athletes. Until this point, I hadn't mentored many teenage boys. My past experience was mostly in mentoring young women.

The day that I accepted her request was the day my career took a sharp detour toward a new, meaningful area in my industry. It marked my first experience with a high schooler who had high hopes of transitioning into college football, parents who had high demands for their son's future, and coaches who, as I learned, were only doing what they thought was best for their player.

I set up a group meeting with this young man's family and a few of my coaching friends, and in minutes of taking a seat in the room, I figured out the main issue. This kid's mom was the dominant parent in the family. She was a warrior who didn't let anything slip past her. The coaches were having a problem trying to get what they wanted out of this lady. They weren't used to dealing with a woman who was the decision-maker of the family.

You know, there are many amazing coaches in this world, but there are also many not-so-amazing coaches. This young man's high school coaches were trying to pry their way into his life, and it was creating a wedge between him and his mother. They tried talking circles around the woman in hopes of getting the young man to accept the college that *they* wanted him to attend. But it was not going to work this way. To settle things, I called in another friend of mine, a therapist. Together, we were able to fix the family's deep-rooted issues, and in the end, the son and mother were able to create an even closer bond.

A second call followed soon after.

"I have a student who's not listening," a woman gasped in disappointment. "He believes school is just about football. He doesn't understand that he needs to focus on his grades as well. Can you come and talk to him?"

This time around, I had a little more knowledge of how things worked with student-athletes and some of the issues they were dealing with. When I met with him, I brought along one of my NFL clients. We explained the importance of education and how the real world worked. The child was under the impression that as long as he was the best player on the field, he didn't need to take school seriously. We made sure he understood that without meeting the requirements for entering college, he wouldn't have a chance to play sports on that level. Once he realized that not going to college also meant his chances of playing in the NFL would be slim to none, it was easy to get him back on track with his grades.

From there, a third call came in with a new request.

"An NFL player wants to give a certain student $500, but he wants the young man to earn it," a friend in the sports business said on the other end of the phone. "He's a sophomore in high school. Can he come volunteer for you for the summer and then you give him the $500 at the end?"

I agreed to take him on, as our community events were kicking off. We welcomed him with a bulk of other volunteers. As the summer went by, the young man and I became extremely close. At the end of his time with us, he asked, "Are you coming to my football game?"

I was shocked. As close as we were, I had no idea he played football. He was such a thin kid that no one would have assumed that he was an athlete.

When I went to support him, I learned that he was one of the top athletes at his school. I met his mother, an older lady in her late sixties. She was amazing. She and I became like family, and we stayed in touch from that day.

As his senior year approached, his mom called and said they were having an issue. "It doesn't look like he's going to be eligible for college football," she said. She didn't fully understand what it meant to be ineligible and asked me to help her figure out what to do. I wasn't going to allow him to end up ineligible.

I immediately went to the website of the National Collegiate Athletic Association (NCAA) and coordinated a meeting with his coach. I was determined to understand what he needed to do in order to go to college. I cared about *that* more than anything. I knew his background and the track he would be headed down if football was removed from his life. If this young man didn't get out of New Orleans, he was going to end up on the street. I knew that getting him into college would be saving his life!

In the end, though, it was up to the child to decide what he wanted to do. He was a star. He had 30 offers from all over the country. He had gotten it into his mind that he didn't need to go to class, that a few F's weren't a problem. Everyone else around him started to panic, but as for me, I was furious. This young man's scholarship and future were on the line, and the high school was still letting him play football every Friday night. His mother was kept completely in the dark. She only knew what the coaches were willing to tell her, so the responsibility for this young man's future fell into our hands. I can say it was only by the grace of God that we got this young man to graduate and go to college.

Through my involvement with the first few student-athletes and their families, I met dozens of others who were in similar situations. Suddenly, I found myself receiving more and more phone calls. I looked over transcripts, checked on grades, double-checked their classes and more. I guided these young men back on track, and I helped them qualify for college. It was my top priority.

The high school football programs in the city started inviting me to speak to their staff and players and conduct transcript audits. Coaches from around the region wanted to meet me and discuss eligibility.

It got out of hand.

For a while, I didn't know what the solution would be. Some of the parents would get upset because I didn't have the time to mentor their sons. The thing is, I was only one person! I hadn't even started a true mentorship program. I stumbled into this responsibility, and I was trying to keep it afloat, meanwhile running my business and recovering from an injury I'd had months before. Despite the circumstances, I was trying to help as many student-athletes as possible.

We started bringing young athletes on tours to different colleges through a non-profit. The goal, for me, was never the NFL. It was how to get these kids out of the worst parts of New Orleans and onto a campus, where they can adapt, graduate, and make something of themselves. Of course, a lot of these kids wouldn't go to college at all if you removed sports. If they could find a way to play football and not go to school, they'd do it in a heartbeat. There-fore, I had to approach it from an angle that was attractive to them. I had to explain to them that there was no way for them to bypass academics and that they needed to have the grades and the right classes in order to keep playing ball. This led me to begin studying under coaches who were eligibility gurus. I researched this subject matter more in-depth. I kept up with the rules, communicated with colleges, spoke to compliance departments, and learned all that I could about what these young men needed to do.

I became a master at it. I could look at a transcript and tell a child and his family exactly what he had to do to become eligible for college sports. As time passed, I struggled with the fact that, after these boys got out of high school and into college, I wouldn't be able to help them as much.

I knew how this field worked, and I knew it wasn't set up to help our young men succeed. I didn't care what anyone tried to tell me. The facts spoke for themselves. It's why nearly eighty percent of them go broke after they retire from the NFL. The system is not structured for them to thrive, so I made sure they could qualify through every loophole and requirement.

I didn't let up. Years later, I decided to become an agent, in hopes of helping prevent young athletes who shift into the NFL from ending their football career broke and broken. Becoming an agent hasn't been all ups. As the industry likes to put it, I had "crossed over to the dark side." People started automatically categorizing me, although I never saw myself as just an agent. That's not all that I am; I'm an advocate.

It has even felt unfair to me that I've had to stop educating high school families because of the frowned upon perception that comes along with the relationship between an agent and high school student-athlete.

Parents are not being taught the art of recruitment and the requirements for participating in college sports. They're still left trying to figure out where to go, who to contact and what to do during their child's early years as an athlete. It's imperative that they are prepared if they want their sons to succeed both in college and in their future careers.

At the end of the day, these boys are entering into business agreements. This entire industry is about paying the right people the right amount of money to get the best players possible. Millions of dollars go into this. Coaches lose their jobs over this. Everything boils down to the dollar. And still, it's the parent's responsibility to get their son into a college.

I know how much of a struggle it can be. My mother was a single mom. There were a lot of things she didn't know, a lot of things she had to learn the hard way and on her own. Nearly 70 percent of football players come from single-mother homes.

I've seen it for myself too many times — moms sitting in football meetings with a lost and confused expression on their faces. It's too easy for them to be taken advantage of by people who don't have their best interests (or their sons' best interests) at heart. For this reason, I say that this is a book for every mom, but that every dad, student-athlete, and coach should read.

Why am I writing this book? To help more families, dedicated parents, coaches, and growing young athletes reach their elite potential. I am here to teach you the steps of eligibility and college recruitment, the psychological components that are missing from most conversations, the reality of this life in sports, and how to best prepare and obtain a future of long-term success and financial stability.

I may not be able to educate high school student-athletes and their families by physically walking them through the process anymore, but this book stands as my solution. It's a solution for helping young men prepare for success in the first seasons of their lives, from eighth through twelfth grade. It's a solution for the next generation of athletes to have a greater opportunity to become the best men that they can be.

1

TAKING RESPONSIBILITY

FIRST, LET'S MAKE something clear. Although a coach's job includes mentoring and nurturing the young men that they manage, they are mostly hired to teach them the skills needed to enhance their performance and to care for them through the football season. Most underprivileged programs and public schools don't have the resources or finances to allow coaches the time to address or plan ahead for their players' personal, psychological, physical, or academic well-being. In the majority of the situations, coaches are there to teach the fundamentals of football and occasionally mentor these young men. That's it.

When it comes to growing and fostering eligibility for higher education, this is not always included or even completely expected of high school coaches. Keep in mind that it can be difficult for those who often have dozens of young men to monitor, to act as both a mentor and coach, especially if they have a job outside of the school.

Coaches can't always do the whole job themselves. The same is true for parents. A coach can teach many valuable lessons, but those lessons must be reinforced by someone in the household. It is the parents' responsibility to ensure the student stays on the right path.

As a parent, you have to be actively involved in your son's life — in sports and in other ways. While a coach may be able to provide a great positive male figure in a young man's life, particularly one who may not have another male figure to look up to, their focus is still largely on the sport.

When your child's grades are beginning to dip, reach out to someone at the school who is outside of the football program — someone who is going to keep you in the loop and help you correct the course for your child's future. You need to be able to take a step back from football for a moment and see where your child is falling short academically. From there, you can start making the changes needed to keep his college eligibility intact.

Eligibility itself can change from year to year, so you have to make sure to keep up. The rules and requirements are completely at the discretion of the NCAA (National Collegiate Athletic Association). Today, in 2018, the core requirement is a 2.3 GPA, whereas before it was a 2.0 GPA. Changes like this are not uncommon, and you must be prepared for them.

Now, a transcript is your child's ticket to their future in college football (NCAA sports). In order to compete in NCAA sports, it is required for student-athletes to complete 16 core courses, which falls under four different categories: math, science, social studies, and English. Therefore, in regards to eligibility, make sure to focus on his core GPA, rather than his cumulative GPA. The NCAA has grade requirements and a timeframe that students must meet as well. Because of this, it's important for your athlete to understand that a class like physical education or art will not count as a core credit for eligibility purposes, whereas math and English classes will. We'll discuss academic eligibility more in-depth in the next chapter.

Thinking Beyond High School

It's so important for parents to take responsibility for their son's success now because they are the only part of the journey that isn't temporary. Once a student-athlete move on to college, they most likely won't keep in contact with their high school football coaches. This means that the next level, and all of its complications, fall back on the parents.

Take these early years to instill in your child the idea that there are things for them outside of football — that college offers more opportunities than just football. Help him to understand that it's healthy and important to have an identity outside of the sport he plays, no matter how good he is on the field. This places him in a better position for long-term success. The reality is, if he enters the NFL, it will be a relatively brief part of his life. Therefore, he will need to have a part of himself that can exist independently of it.

This is where the parent's role is vital. Sit down with your son and guide him in figuring out the various aspects of his options going forward. Allow him to figure out what parts of school he likes and dislikes, his gifts and talents, and his strengths and weaknesses. This can be essential in securing his future and provide a sort of "safety net," a backup plan for when football isn't the main part of his life.

Coaches and their philosophies can change everything in an instant. For example, a young man who was formerly a starting player can be replaced with the introduction of a new coach and a new team plan. Just in case, it's important to have something for him to fall back on. This will keep him from feeling like his life and his identity are falling apart if things don't hold up on the field. Give him something to live for and strive for outside of football. Teach him not only to be a great player but also to be a great man. He'll be educated and ready to adapt to the next stages of his life.

Eight Responsibility Tips

This is a huge order for any parent, but it's an important part of ensuring not only your child's future but also your legacy. Pay attention to your child. Know what he's good at in multiple areas and teach him to be responsible for his academics. When it comes to keeping track of eligibility, here are eight useful tips to help you along the way:

1. Meet with a counselor and your son before and after each semester so you can go over his schedule and keep track of his progress in terms of how it aligns with the NCAA

requirements.

2. If your son gets hurt or injured in a game or practice, go to the doctor! Step in and ensure he heals before allowing him to jump back on the field. Too often minor injuries go ignored and untreated until they become major health issues in the future.

3. Maintain relationships with your son's teachers. Be sure to get their email addresses and check in with them periodically. This allows your child to stay on top of what he's doing and it keeps you in the loop as well. Having a good relationship with a teacher can also be helpful if your child stumbles a bit along the way. A good teacher will work with you when he or she realizes how involved and invested you are in your child's education.

4. Without being overbearing, talk to his coaches. Coaches are going to be a huge part of your child's life, so it's important to see what they're seeing and know what they know. Ask his coaches for updates on his progress. Ask where he can improve.

5. Try to go to multiple university Junior Days early. Even if your son is a freshman, it can be extremely helpful to attend and

see what universities have to offer. You can speak with representatives from universities and use their help to figure out what your child needs to do to meet their standards of eligibility. Some universities may be looking for certain electives, so meeting with a representative and counselor can help you tailor your child's educational track to whichever university he wants to attend.

6. Try to get him an internship. The value of hard work is limitless, and an internship can be a life-changing thing for many students. Call some local companies and have him pick from among them, as he would do with a top-five in sports. Ask him about a career he might see himself doing in the future, then help him explore every avenue of that industry. Once he finds something that he likes, you can start helping him look into the requirements for it and which degree he would need to pursue. This process will also help him narrow down the universities to pick from and give him something else to look forward to beyond his ambitions for football.

7. Have him read self-help books. Books that deal with issues like helping other people

and having healthy growth and a healthy personality can be life-changing for young people. Your son may very well be walking into a celebrity lifestyle within a few years, so giving him the tools he needs to lead a happy and healthy life can be essential to his future. Fame can change a person entirely and even bring on depression. Being aware of who he is at his core can keep him from getting swept up in a crowd that may not be the best for him.

8. Get him involved in the community. Have him volunteer with local non-profit organizations and learn the importance of giving back.

Too often athletes reach their mid-twenties and early thirties, retire from the NFL, having never held a job, gone through an interview, or even created a resume, and suffer from culture shock. This can lead to an overwhelming amount of stress and debt and leave him completely unprepared to deal with hardship and hard work of the real world.

Keeping the eight responsibility tips at the forefront of your mind, year after year, will prepare your son for success on the field and off of it. At a young age, he'll know how to exist in a world where he's not merely an athlete. He'll have a career in mind, know his skills, have a solid attitude, healthy self-image, be willing to give back to his community and hold long-term goals for his future. When he hits adulthood and suddenly finds himself at a crossroad, he'll be ready to take the path that's right for him.

2

GETTING
EDUCATED

IF YOU HAVE the preconception that what you don't know can't hurt you, you're in for a rude awakening. Knowledge is power, and what you don't know can *absolutely* hurt you, especially when it comes to the sports industry. To begin preparing for your son's future, it's imperative that you become knowledgeable of the National Collegiate Athletic Association (NCAA).

The NCAA is the boss of all bosses (or better yet, the dictatorship) for your son's entire college sports experience. On their website ncaa.org, you'll find an abundance of information for student-athletes and collegiate sports, including a breakdown of the players' rules, regulations, and eligibility to play and maintain success. For example, it currently states that if a student fails the NCAA regulated test for a performance-enhancing drug (PED), he loses one full year of eligibility for the first offense (25 percent of their total eligibility) and are withheld from competition for 365 days from the date of the test. A second positive test for a PED results in the loss of all remaining eligibility. This organization stands as a central place for checks and balances. They determine what's fair and what's not for the industry, including the rules that govern the coaches and overall game.

The amount of information found on the NCAA website can quickly make you feel overwhelmed, but the beauty of this organization is that they offer great assistance. There's a hotline number you can call for immediate help. In a matter of minutes, you'll be able to reach someone willing to answer specific questions for you.

All in all, *before* your son reaches college, one of the first steps to educating yourself will be visiting ncaa.org and familiarizing yourself with their hub. The key to growth and improvement is to continue learning. However, you don't have to conquer the entire website in one day. Visit it over time, ideally throughout your son's first years of high school. As you do, you can turn to *A Simple Guide for Navigating NCAA.org*, added to the appendix of this book, to help you along the way.

Academic Eligibility

In Chapter 1, we briefly covered the meaning of a core GPA and a cumulative GPA. In this chapter, we'll dive into why you should focus your attention on one over the other. A cumulative GPA is what's used to qualify your son to graduate from high school, but a core GPA is what's used to determine his eligibility to play an NCAA sport. The two are totally different.

You can have a child who is eligible to graduate from high school but doesn't qualify to play football in college. While a high school cumulative GPA minimum graduation requirement might be 1.5, the NCAA currently states that an entering student-athlete must reach the threshold of a minimum 2.3 core GPA to be eligible to compete in his first year of college. Therefore, if *Student A* has a cumulative GPA of 2.79 and a core GPA of 1.9, he's eligible to graduate but not eligible to play college football. On the other hand, if *Student B* has a cumulative GPA of 2.79 and a core of 2.33, he will not only graduate high school but also be completely cleared to play college football. (Please keep in mind that some universities require a higher core GPA, and the 2.3 core GPA is a minimum.)

According to NCAA.org:

- Beginning August 1, 2016, you must earn *at least* a 2.300 GPA in NCAA core courses to be eligible to compete in your first year of college.
- To get a scholarship and practice with the team, you must earn *at least* a 2.000 GPA in NCAA core courses.

Cumulative is the summary of the final grade of every class, whereas the core is only the sum of NCAA approved core courses. In other words, elective classes such as art, physical education, music, and home economics would not be included in the final core GPA. Most students plan to get easy A's in their elective classes, and if they do so, that's great — but it's only great for their cumulative GPA. Getting A's in elective classes won't push a core GPA any higher, and having this mindset can eventually hinder their chances of playing sports in college.

So, what are considered core courses and how many credits are available at a high school? The NCAA deems classes in English, math, natural or physical science, social science, foreign language, and comparative religion or philosophy courses as core. However, the number of credits available depends on what classes the high school has to offer and how the high school categorizes certain classes. In most cases, high schools offer a wide variety of NCAA approved core options. For instance, some high schools will offer a credit in speech or creative writing classes that may be classified as an NCAA approved English core. The number of core credits obtained will be up to your son's school and his counselor's discretion, although (as stated in Chapter 1) there must be at least 16 core credits completed by his senior year to qualify for the NCAA. You'll find that taking additional core classes, beyond the minimum requirement, helps boost the core GPA.

To begin narrowing down which core courses your son will plan to take over the years, visit the NCAA Eligibility Center and click on the high school portal. Once on the portal, click the "List of NCAA Courses" (formerly known as Form 48-H) tab above. Input your son's six-digit High School Code or six-digit CEEB/ACT Code or search for his school by name. Once accessed, you should find a full list of core courses available at the bottom of the page. If you have trouble finding this information, call the NCAA toll-free hotline number (877-622-2321) to get answers.

Recently, the NCAA released a new rule that states, "Ten of the sixteen core courses must be completed before the start of the student-athlete's seventh semester of high school and at least seven of these ten core courses must be in English, math, or natural or physical science." In layman's terms, ten of the core courses that your son takes between his freshman year of high school and the summer of his junior year are locked in. "Locked in" meaning that those core courses cannot be retaken to improve his core grade-point average.

Before this limiting rule existed, it was possible for student-athletes to take any of their core courses as many times as possible in order to get a better grade. For instance, if a student had ended his freshman, sophomore and junior years with D's in his core courses, he would've been able to retake those classes in the summer months before his senior year in an effort to raise his core GPA. However, going forward, this is no longer the case. As explained, ten of the core courses finished between his freshman and junior years would be locked in for good. In this example, the student-athlete's only option would be to consider taking additional core courses in an attempt to score higher grades and raise his core GPA.

As you can see, rules can change fast within the NCAA. Staying up to date with what's new and aware of what is standard is extremely important, and it's best to stay on top of things from the beginning!

If you find that your son has gotten to the end of his senior year with a core GPA lower than 2.3, there won't be much you can do — it'd be too late to revive it. This is the reason I stress that what you do now will make the greatest difference in your son's longevity and success in the future. Once you've learned the NCAA requirements, you will be able to address issues seamlessly, year by year, and not have to attempt to suddenly fix everything before your son's graduation.

Here's my best advice for you: don't get discouraged! Again, this is why you are starting as early as possible. You want to take out time to truly understand how all of this stuff works. Remember to also have consistent open dialogue sessions with your son's counselor. (*I can't mention this enough.*) If a counselor isn't open to working with you cohesively, don't be afraid to talk it over with their boss or principal, because, at the end of the day, this is about your child's life!

I've personally dealt with counselors in the past who were not concerned about the future of their student-athletes. There was one lady who had reached her limit with talking with me about a student-athlete's eligibility and said, "My responsibility is not to make sure he's qualified for the NCAA. My responsibility as his counselor is for me to ensure he graduates according to the state requirements." My response to her was straight-forward. "Well then, you shouldn't be dealing with student-athletes at all," I said.

This counselor had put the student on a curriculum track for entrepreneurship, which was a path the school had constructed as they did for all the students there. Well, according to this "track," the student I was working with was supposed to take a set of electives instead of other core classes. This was terrible for his NCAA eligibility, but she wouldn't allow him to change out of an elective to add a core because his "track" hadn't listed it as a requirement. When I heard this was going on, I immediately contacted the principal and made a complaint. This young man had a scholarship on the line, meaning free education for a black man whose family truly needed it. I was not going to allow this counselor to stand in the way of his opportunity.

Why hadn't they implemented a track for athletes to succeed in college? Why had this school created a "track" system for everyone but athletes? You cannot obtain a scholarship for going to college to be an entrepreneur, but you *can* receive a scholarship for athletics. Why not provide a track that positions student-athletes to be successful both on and off the field? This was the question that stuck in my mind while dealing with this counselor. I knew this was the same young man who was helping to fill their stadium seats every Friday night and putting money back into the school. It was backward not to consider his needs.

In the end, the counselors who are willing to go the extra mile, be supportive of student-athletes, take time to understand NCAA eligibility, and push for scholarship success in this area will be so happy to see those young men graduate from college or make it to the NFL. And it's because of these counselors that successful athletes and college graduates return to visit their schools, host events, and give back.

Although, as a parent, you may not be able to always rely on school counselors to know or be concerned about academic eligibility requirements for your student-athlete, there's no need to feel overwhelmed or stressed. As a matter of fact, decide now not to let the small details stress you. To narrow down some of the information poured out thus far, simply concentrate on helping your son obtain the highest GPA possible, receiving nothing under a C. That's it. When you focus on helping your child achieve the best grades in all of his classes, at all times, it'll relieve some of the pressure you may be feeling from the load of information.

However, be careful with thinking that earning C's are okay. Too many C's can possibly make your son ineligible. For example, if a student has all C's in his required core classes, he will end up with a 2.0 core GPA, which is below the NCAA's GPA requirement. This would deem him ineligible to compete in his first year of college.

————

Now, let's take it a step further. The NCAA core GPA requirement only covers one side of the coin. The other side of academic eligibility you must consider is the SAT/ACT test score requirement. First, you must understand how standardized test scores coordinate with GPA requirements for the NCAA. According to ncaa.org, Division 1 uses a sliding scale to match SAT/ACT scores and core-course grade-point averages to determine eligibility. The sliding scale is created to balance your son's test scores with his core GPA. In other words, if he has a low core GPA, he will need a high SAT or ACT test score to be eligible. On the other hand, if he has a high GPA, he can afford to have a lower test score and still pass through eligibility.

Here is a short example of the current NCAA sliding scale (for those planning to attend a Division

1 college or university for the 2018/2019 or 2019/
2020 academic year):

Core GPA	SAT*	ACT Sum*
3.5	430	39
3.3	550	44
3.0	720	52
2.7	800	58
2.5	900	68
2.3	980	75
A combined SAT score is calculated by adding reading and math subscores. An ACT sum score is calculated by adding English, math, reading and science subscores. For the full sliding scale, visit www.eligibilitycenter.org.		

As you can see, focusing on your son obtaining the highest core GPA possible can pay off in a major way, especially if he's not a great standardized test-taker. For parents who can afford to hire a tutor, I highly recommend it. In order to avoid dealing with unbelievable pressures during your son's junior and senior years, start preparing him mentally and emotionally to see the value in paying attention in each of his classes, finishing all homework assignments, studying early for tests, and so on. For academic eligibility, there is *a lot* riding on his final core GPA. The sooner he recognizes this, the better.

Scholarships

What about athletic scholarships? Do they automatically fall on the laps of high school players with good grades?

Not at all.

There has to be a mutual agreement between the university and the student. Years ago, I worked with a young man who had amazing grades; he passed academic eligibility with flying colors on paper, but there were no universities interested in offering him an athletic scholarship. You see, the athletic interest has to be completely mutual. Coaches show signs of interest by sending an "offer" to a student-athlete. In turn, this offer yields athletic scholarships.

However, all offers are not the same. In the collegiate realm, coaches have deemed a difference between what they see as a "committable" offer and a "non-committable" offer.

When parents understand this difference, it changes the game. Coaches will never outright tell you whether an offer is committable or non-committable. They will only express that they are "offering" your son.

Now, let's break down the details of a "committable" and "non-committable" offer and how you can tell the difference between the two.

A "non-committable" offer is simply a university's way of letting a student-athlete know that the coach and the university are interested and would like to evaluate him more to determine if they want to accept a commitment from him. This doesn't automatically mean the coach is not going to accept your son's commitment in the future. It simply means he likes him enough to give an "offer" and want to see more before moving forward with a commitment. The best way to look at "non-committable" offers is to see them as simply signs of interest. (In other words, it's like a man telling a woman that he wants to date her but has not yet determined if he wants to *marry* her.)

On the other hand, a "committable" offer has more potential. It's when a school "offers" a student-athlete and is ready to accept the student-athlete's commitment. In order to ensure an athletic scholarship and a place on that college football team, the student-athlete *must* say he wants to commit and the school *must* accept. (This is what I mean by having a mutual agreement and a school accepting a commitment from a student-athlete. It's like a man proposing and waiting on the woman to accept.) If this occurs, trust me, you do not want your son to wait around too long, weighing other options, before making a decision to commit to a particular school. Things can change very quickly for coaches who have spots to fill.

Now, if a school rejects your son's commitment, it is a sign that it was a "non-committable" offer, and at that point, he must move on to his next offer. He must recognize that universities and coaches have the power to choose not to honor an offer, due to the fact that they are not binding. In addition, a student-athlete can "decommit" from a school and reopen his recruitment process. Again, commitments are not binding until an NLI is signed (which we will discuss further into this chapter).

Nonetheless, there are ways to influence a "non-committable" offer of interest to become a sure, authentic offer of commitment. How so? Well, in most cases, it is an unwritten rule that the high school student-athlete with an offer must attend that university's camp. Coaches want to see potential players in action — operating right in front of them on the field, competing against others, seeing how they handle coaching, and cooperating with a team. Some believe a film clip, despite how impressive it might be, does not do justice. Therefore, the best chance of a student-athlete influencing a "non-committable" offer to become a "committable" offer is to show up in person at the university's camp.

KEY TAKEAWAYS

How to know the difference between a committable offer and a non-committable offer?

- If your son tries to commit to a school that has offered him and the school rejects his commitment, this is a sign that it was a "non-committable" offer. Your son cannot play for this school. He must move on to his next offer.
- If your son tries to commit to a school that has offered him and the school accepts his commitment, this is a sign that it was a "committable" offer, and your son can play for this school.

You may be wondering: *What do I do if my son has ten offers? How can I possibly bring him to all ten college camps?* You don't have to bring him to all ten, but make his presence known to as many as you can afford to bring him to. Here's a rule of thumb: narrow his list of offers down to his top five choices. If he's serious about committing, you *must* get him to each of those five camps; otherwise, there is a large chance (most likely over a sixty percent chance) that he will not be accepted or granted an athletic scholarship by a school he has not visited.

National Letter of Intent

When your son has decided on the school he would like to attend and the school has accepted such commitment, this is like marriage. This is where a National Letter of Intent, also known as an NLI, comes into play. The NLI is a binding agreement between the prospective student-athlete and college. By signing an NLI, the student-athlete agrees to attend the college for one academic year and in exchange that college agrees to provide athletics financial aid for one academic year. (It's important to add here that scholarships are a year-by-year deal, just as the NLI.)

Again, I want to emphasize that getting educated early is key. Staying updated on the NCAA's ever-changing rules and regulations, keeping track of your son's core GPA from the very start of his freshman year, understanding the world of offers and athletic scholarships, and ensuring you are consistently attentive to his academic needs, will lead to undeniable results.

3

INVESTING IN YOUR CHILD

INVESTING IN YOUR child is crucial.

Football can be a very costly sport, and saving money early eliminates a lot of stress and frustration. Expenses can start as early as his pee wee football years. In New Orleans, my hometown, children start as early as five years old. (Yes, we have kids here who are playing football and learning the dynamics of the game before they even reach kindergarten.) If you have a son who shows interest in football early, there's a high chance he will want to play in middle school and high school, and there's a possibility he'll play in college. My advice is for you to start saving money immediately — especially single mothers and those who are on fixed incomes. You will need to save a substantial amount of money for the football career your son desires to achieve.

I suggest you go as far as creating a bank account for your son or another safe place where you put money aside and treat as if it doesn't exist — even if it's only $20 ($5 a week) or $40 a month. Through the years, you'll have to buy gear, pay football program fees, enroll him in summer football camps, make college visits, pay for summer school, pay for training, take care of injuries, etc. It can be expensive and having a prepared stash to pull from will pay off in the long run.

Remember to be realistic about what you set aside because when you try to save an unrealistic abundance, you're more likely to keep going back to it for things you need personally. Save an amount you won't miss being taken, and continue to do this year after year. Before you know it, you may have $8,000 saved by the time your son reaches high school and even more when he reaches college. If he doesn't get the scholarship you're expecting for college, it won't hold him back. You'll have extra money aside to jumpstart him his first year. Now, let's say he does get the scholarship. You'll be able to use that extra money as a down payment for a car or use it for other things he'll need for college. However it's used, it'll be money you can invest in your child when he needs it most.

If your student-athlete is looking to play Division 1, the majority of your expenses will go toward years of traveling to campuses and visiting football camps to help him get exposure. Some student-athletes will want the opportunity to showcase their talents and gain experience by competing on other teams, such as 7-on-7 tournament teams, which also requires a lot of traveling.

Here's what you must understand: you can either choose to start gradually saving toward investing in your child now or be forced to invest in your child when the expenses show up. There's no way around it. If your son is naturally talented, you'll want to push him to play on the next level, give him the opportunities and exposure he deserves, and be prepared for anything that comes his way. So, get ahead of the curve now and avoid being left with the stress of financial pressures every year.

Investing in Medical Treatment

Investing in your child also includes giving your son the right medical treatment early on. I knew a student-athlete who he had an ankle injury back when he was playing youth football, and today, he's a junior in high school with that same ankle injury. For years, it went without being properly cared for, and every time he had a crash on the field, he added to the problem. Now, I've heard that he's suffering the consequences and his college recruitment status is on the line.

If your child is letting you know that any part of his body hurts, go get it checked! Invest right at that moment, and don't ignore it. You'd have to pay more if the problem worsens later.

I know of another student-athlete who complained to his mom about his hip hurting all season. The mom didn't rush to go take care of it, and he continued playing football, running and crashing into other players on the field. One morning the young man woke up in a condition they never expected — he was no longer able to walk. They panicked, rushing him to the hospital afraid he was paralyzed. Later that evening, they learned he'd fractured his hip a while back, but because it was never cared for, it had fully broken. Today, he has a rod in his hip, all because his parents didn't take his pain seriously the moment the injury occurred. (I'll add that even if the child doesn't complain but you're aware of an injury, go get it checked out anyway.)

Getting proper medical treatment, hiring a trainer, and getting your son regular massages are all investments that can help them compete today and endure strong into the future.

Investing in Football Camps

Another part of investing in your child is getting them to university football camps, which I'll give more details about in Chapter 6. Camps are some of the most important evaluation tools coaches use for recruiting. For instance, coaches will even take a player's camp evaluation over his highlight tape; that's just how crucial they are to attend.

College satellite camps, where football coaches from different universities come together to host a camp, give student-athletes a great opportunity to compete on different levels and get recognized for their talents. Average football camps will range from $35-$55, while most major football camps, usually held for multiple days at a time, will range from $300-$500 or more.

There are also special-designed camps just for quarterbacks, running backs, wide receivers and tight ends that can start around $700. Again, whether you're buying cleats, paying a yearly football budget fee for high school, paying for medical treatment, or hiring a tutor, you can't get around investing in your child's football career if you want him to succeed. This is why using the tips given for saving money early is imperative to build a promising future for your son.

Tips for Saving & Raising Money

Let's go over several saving tips (some were already mentioned in this chapter), as well as ways you can begin fundraising money:

- Allocate a small amount of money each month, whether that's $20 a paycheck or more. Put it in a separate bank account, named as College Fund or Athletic Fund.
- Save funds from your income tax refund each year.
- If you have a large family, do a family fundraiser. You can keep it as simple as sending out a mass text message to your family members that says, "My son's football budget is $500. I'd love for you guys to help by donating what you can." Before you know it, everyone's $20 – $30 gifts will build to make the budget.
- Carpool to games with other parents when you can.
- Instead of buying all brand-new gear, con-

sider finding secondhand gear that your son may not mind wearing. Some teens may complain, but if he doesn't care, this can be a reasonable option for saving money for his future.

- Don't brush aside your son's high school football program fundraisers. Ensure you join him in fully participating and raising as much as possible.

Saving money is simplistic. The most important step is figuring out which saving strategies work best for your situation. The worst thing you can do is ignore this and try to find the money you need at the last minute. In order to ensure your son has the tools, flexibility, treatment, and exposure he needs to propel forward year after year, you must start saving today.

4

NETWORKING

MEETING YOUR SON'S future coaches can be a breeze when you're in the right place at the right time and with the right questions. Although the end goal is always the same when networking, there are multiple ways you can approach it, depending on whether your son is headed to high school or headed to college.

Headed to High School

For those entering high school, there will usually be an open house or orientation held at the beginning of the school year. You can use this opportunity to meet the coaches, get their contact information, and ask in-depth questions about their school. If you can't make it to the orientation, call and ask to schedule a tour of the school on another day or leave a message for the A.D. (Athletic Director) to get back to you.

During a visit, you'll be able to speak with the coaches as well as spend quality time with the principal, teachers, and counselors. When speaking with a counselor, be sure to specifically discuss the school's athletes. Ask how many of their athletes normally move on to Division 1 colleges. Ask about their knowledge of the NCAA and how the rules relate to a student-athlete's core and cumulative GPA. Ensure the counselor also fully explains options and resources your son will have if he ever falls behind in his classes.

Learn about the high school's options for student-athletes who are interested in graduating early, mid-year. Mid-year graduates graduate from high school in December, instead of May, of their senior year and enroll in college in January. If you believe your son is mature enough for a mid-year graduation, I suggest moving in that direction. Why? Because graduating mid-year has its benefits. It gives student-athletes the opportunity to learn the college football playbook early, get in shape, and possibly earn a starting position. It also helps student-athletes adjust to college life and make a smooth transition.

Headed to College

For those entering college, there are multiple opportunities to sit down and talk with a coach, such as Junior Day, official visits, unofficial visits, and football camps. (Don't worry. We'll discuss everything you should know about these types of visits in Chapter 6.) Before engaging with college coaches for the first time, do a little research. Seek out which schools they've attended in the past and learn the names of their head coaches. As I stated in the last chapter, it's smart to Google them and find them on social media.

Social media has been a true breakthrough for the athletic world. There are some coaches who love connecting with parents via Twitter or Facebook more than anything else. You can easily introduce yourself and your son, let them know you are considering coming to their school, and ask if it's possible for you two to meet at the school to discuss the football program. Again, *some* coaches are open to this type of communication but not all.

As you begin the networking process for college,

you must understand that the coaches have NCAA rules to follow as well when it comes to recruiting. The NCAA created a recruiting calendar that dictates when and how coaches are to contact recruits. One rule, in particular, you must be aware of is that they are not allowed to initiate contact by approaching, calling, emailing or visiting a recruit before September 1 of their junior year. Only if an underclassman (freshman and sophomore high schooler) is on campus for a football camp, Junior Day or an unofficial visit will a coach be allowed to make temporary contact. On the other hand, if the athlete initiates the contact with the coach, they can talk.

The goal is to start building a strong, positive network within football programs early on. When a coach is familiar with your friendly face and casual conversation, he will be open to sharing more information and offering more assistance than what's expected of him. In high school, this will set your son up for success — in college, growing this open line of communication, through an early focus on networking, will make it that much easier for interested coaches to make a final decision to recruit your son. If your son is dreaming of playing sports on the collegiate level, you both need to get busy!

The Art of Approach

The main lesson in networking can be summed up in three words: reputation, relationship, and respect. It doesn't matter whether a coach is working at a small high school or a prestigious university, if you cross his path, get to know him and treat him with respect. If you remember anything from this book, remember to treat *all* coaches with dignity, despite their current status or your opinion of how they operate. Why? Because coaches have a tight circle. They talk amongst each other, and their positions of power can elevate quickly. The man who is your son's coach today may become a coordinator for the NFL, a coach for an NFL team, or the head coach of a college in the future. You never know where he may end up or where your son will be in the near future, so it's best not to ruin the relationship.

To prove my point, I'll tell you two stories, each of a student who left a bad taste in a coach's mouth and then went on to regret it years later.

A past NFL client of mine had gotten into a terrible argument with his coach back in college. Nearly eight years into his NFL career, the team decided to hire the very same coach. Do you know what happened next? They couldn't get along. They bumped heads so much that the team eventually cut him from the team. Prematurely, he lost his position in the NFL over issues he hadn't let go of since college. It was painful to watch, but it was even more painful for him to experience.

Another young man was a high school athlete who received a pretty good offer from a university. Although extremely talented, his arrogance quickly got him in trouble. "I'm about to blow up!" he thought. He thought that he was about to receive more offers as well as bigger offers from bigger schools "This offer isn't good enough for me. I know I'll be picked by a better school than this." Well, with that mindset, he didn't see an issue with completely ignoring the coach who sent the offer. Every time the coach would reach out, he turned a deaf ear and didn't respond. And guess what happened sometime after? That "better" school he was waiting on never showed up with an offer. He believed he was such a big shot that he could ignore offers without even giving a courteous response. You see, he could've at least communicated by saying, "Hey, coach, I love your program. I love what you're doing, but my family and I are considering going in a different direction." Instead, he burnt the bridge between him and the coach by not acknowledging the offer at all, and by the end of his senior year, he was left empty-handed.

In desperation, he tried to revive his relationship with the coach before graduating from high school, but the coach wouldn't respond to his text or phone calls. Now, I actually knew the coach personally so I decided to reach out to see what was really going on. My conversation with the coach confirmed my thought process about the predicament this young man had put himself in. The coach had moved on and was left with a bad taste in his mouth about him. As far as he was concerned, this kid was an egotistical and selfish young man, and he would rather sign someone with a better attitude. So, as you can predict, things didn't end well for this kid. He had to settle for a much smaller football program.

When a coach has his mind made up about a student's character, he shares that information. His words carry weight across programs and eventually affects the student's reputation.

These stories are examples of what you *don't* want to happen in your son's career. Whenever you feel as if a coach is mishandling you or your son, don't react disrespectfully and ensure your son follows suit. As difficult as it might seem, it's best to back away without burning the bridge. By no means am I saying not to address a coach if he gets out of hand. In that case, handle the situation as professionally as possible. However, regardless of the coach's character flaws, he will have to respect you and your son for years to come.

Starting today, teach your student-athlete the

power of reputation and respect as well as the art of his approach, and he'll know how to properly network and build relationships in this industry.

5

CHOOSING
THE RIGHT
HIGH SCHOOL

CHOOSING THE RIGHT high school for your child is paramount to his future success, not only as an athlete but also as a well-rounded individual. As in any sport, there must be a game plan in place. Those four years will combine to create an outcome that, if done correctly, will ensure your child's stability. As a parent, you must organize that plan and pick a high school where your student-athlete will be able to enjoy and thrive — on and off the field.

One of the most important things to consider

when choosing a high school is your child's comfort. Grasp the school's culture, and ask yourself, *Will my child fit in it?* A strong body is dependent on a strong mind, and your child will have to navigate that duality with as much ease in this transition as possible. Choosing a high school where he feels comfortable, wanted, and involved will propel him further than anything else.

When it comes to the school's academic benefits, you want to get answers to the right questions: Are teachers able or willing to help outside of the classroom? What academic resources are available to those who need them? Is tutoring available? Is summer school available? If your child has special needs or a learning disability, which high school has the best resources available to help him? Is there anything in place that helps student-athletes specifically? Ask questions to parents of students currently at the school and get their perspective on things as well. Your child will not be able to meet their college dreams without a good, well-rounded high school education. These questions can help guide you towards a high school where your student-athlete will be able to excel intellectually.

Athletically, you want to get to know the ambitions of the coaches and the culture of the team. Ask the coaches questions about their goals. How do they manage playing time? Are practices and games videotaped? How active are they in educating their players about college recruitment? How many of their players have gone on to play college sports? Starting such conversations is a great first step in locating the best school for your son.

How a high school approaches sports, as well as education, will determine your child's second home for the next four years. If you choose wrong, you may not be able to choose again without a cost. In states like Louisiana, it is illegal to transfer from one school to another for football purposes and still be eligible to play. He is required to sit out on playing football for at least one year. (*Note that the rules vary by state.*)

Let's say you choose *High School A*. Your child is not happy being a benchwarmer there. He wants to switch to *High School B*, one where he will be able to start immediately. Unfortunately, because the decision to switch was made for a football purpose, he may be ineligible to play for at least one year and, in high school sports, one year is a lifetime. It can make or break a future career. To prevent this from happening, it is imperative that you find out your state and region's regulations pertaining to transfers and make an informed decision. (Ask the coaches. Find out what they recommend.)

This stage of gathering information is crucial. This is the time to drill an athletic department with questions and a principal with inquiries. Making an informed decision will pay off tremendously in the end and make all the difference for your student-athlete while he is in high school.

The Challenge of Transitioning

No matter which school you choose, the transition from middle school to high school can be challenging for any young student-athletes. As an eighth grader and one of the oldest on a middle school team, your son was probably a strong, fierce player on the field, but now joining a high school team, he has become one of the youngest and least-experienced players. He may be sitting on the bench, waiting for the starting juniors and seniors to give him a turn. It is a challenging process — one that the quarterback in the previous story had to deal with. This can easily lead to depression in teens.

High school is a challenging season. A student-athlete will be struggling to show their coach who they are. His body will be changing. He will be building muscles in order to compete with the juniors and seniors. He will realize he cannot just practice on Saturdays anymore; he must go to football practice after school every day. He realizes he still has homework to do after those football practices. He'll be juggling more and therefore need more attention.

So, how can you help your child navigate during this time of transition? Prepare him. Help him see that building stamina now only keeps him ahead of the game. Let him know that in any minute a coach can call on him to take the place of a junior or senior. Encourage him to push through those times he may have to study for a big test the day of a big game. Prepare him for peer pressure, for heartache, for hard but rewarding years. He's growing up, and the first year of high school may be the most shocking for him. You'll want him to be able to trust and confide in you and talk to you about his issues with his team, coaches, teachers, or friends. Therefore, keep an open line of communication with him, and, without a doubt, he will be able to transition smoothly.

The Team Structure

To avoid choosing a high school football program that doesn't match well with your son, look at how the team is structured. Ideally, you want your child to play as soon as possible. You need to look at the team's roster and what position each person plays, as well as what year they are. If a team has seven wide receivers with most of them being upperclassmen, your child will most likely sit out his freshman year. However, if another high school has a team with only three wide receivers and only one senior amongst them, the chances of your child playing his freshman year improve dramatically. If you want him to be able to actively play all four years, the second high school will more than likely give your son what he's looking for. Understand that productivity and character will also play a large role when your son hits the field, so you must be realistic with your expectations.

I remember the son of a close friend of mine had a classmate who was a quarterback; however, their high school football team was not known for throwing the ball much. As a result, this young man couldn't do much with his team, neither could he complain to the coach about it. It's not likely for a coach who has been winning with a team to change everything around for one player. This quarterback should have been aware of the school's playing style when he and his parents chose it. He was unhappy, and eventually, things got worse.

One day, this young man's coach said, "Well, we don't think you're a quarterback anymore. We're going to convert you to a defensive back." The coach was not willing to change their playing style for him, and can you guess what happened next? This young man and his parents decided to leave the school.

When he switched high schools for football purposes, he was ineligible to play at his new school for
one year. He essentially lost two of his four years as a
football player — which leads back to the fact that he
did not choose the high school that would best nur-
ture his talents. Think wisely about your choices.

Now, also understand that sitting isn't bad either.
In some cases, student-athletes do not adjust swiftly
enough to play as a freshman, and this is okay.
Therefore, do not pick a school solely on your child
having the opportunity to play. Be aware that an
"opportunity" is just that — an opportunity. It's not a
guarantee. Be realistic, and in most cases, be patient.

Of course, problems occur no matter what, but
reducing those problems by being prepared, knowledgeable, and active in your student-athletes life will
help you and your child achieve the dreams you both
set out with.

Peer Pressure

No matter what school you end up choosing, the
peer pressure, drugs, and alcohol will be a constant
possibility. A number of student-athletes fall into
bad crowds. Drugs and alcohol can cloud their
minds, make them lose focus, and lead them down
an unpromising path. When choosing a high school,

be mindful of your child's ability to handle peer pressure. If you believe your child may easily give in to the pressure, consider a school that has stricter rules and programs governing drugs and alcohol, on or off campus.

Moms, you must be ready to tackle problems as they come. Conversations about drugs and alcohol have to happen, as well as about dating and relationships. Your child will be surrounded by new people at whichever school you choose, and it will be important to grasp the full culture.

The Personality

Coaches are human first. Keep this in mind when you're choosing a high school. If your son has a type-A personality and you put him under a coach who also has a type-A personality, there will be major issues. Two people are highly aggressive, controlling, impatient and have an unrealistic sense of urgency won't flow well together. When you're meeting with coaches, get to know their personality. Since you know your son extremely well already, you'll know how he'll work with coaches. You should be able to recognize who your son is going to get along with or constantly argue with. If your child is sensitive (more of a type-B personality), he probably won't be able to handle the pressure of a coach who yells a lot. This type of student-athlete needs to be with a calmer coach so that he can adapt and grow under him. If not, this type of child will only shut down. Properly teaming up a coach and an athlete always goes back to the personality of the personnel.

What happens if the coaches change in the middle of his high school years and it's no longer a good match? Well, given the circumstance, it'll be time to talk to your son about making adjustments in his personality traits. Now that he has matured some, he should be able to learn how to fall in line no matter who is coaching him.

Recognize that no school experience will be flawless, as no time on the field is without a misstep. The only way to properly navigate your son's school years is by developing a game plan early on, weighing the variables, asking the right questions, and doing everything in your power to choose a place that *fits* your son. Through this process, you and your child will develop an effective way forward.

6

INSIDE
JUNIOR DAY &
FOOTBALL
CAMP

OVER THE YEARS, College Football Junior Days have become an extremely popular and powerful tool for coaches to recruit potential players. Junior Days are scheduled at universities as recruiting events for student-athletes all over the country to visit. Recruits and their parents have to pay their way for this special, one-day opportunity to learn about the university's educational and football programs and campus, as well as meet the coaching staff. In some cases, student-athletes are also allowed to meet the academic advisers or program representatives.

The first step in planning to attend a Junior Day with your son is to go online to the university's website and search for the athletic department's calendar of events, where you should find the date of their scheduled, open-to-the-public Junior Day. Universities typically host their Junior Days around spring football. If you have a difficult time finding the date online, don't hesitate to call the university's recruiting department, saying: "Hey, I'm a mom of a student-athlete. I'm interested in bringing him to your Junior Day. Is it an invite-only event or is it open to the public?"

Understand that most Junior Days are invite-only, so do not get offended if a college informs you that their Junior Day is private. Say thank you, and move on to the next college on your list. If you cannot reach an individual in the recruiting department, simply try to contact one of the coaches directly.

Coaches normally send informal invites (which is usually a verbal invitation through high school coaches) to student-athletes who are high-profile juniors or high-profile sophomores going into their junior year.

> ### KEY TAKEAWAYS
>
> - Coaches are not allowed by the NCAA to initiate contact with recruits until September 1 of their junior year, so this is one of the first ways they will try to get a student-athlete they're interested in on campus.
> - Keep in mind that your son *does not* have to be a junior or receive an invitation to attend this event.

Once you get the date of the public Junior Day, find out the cost for the lunch provided. As mentioned before, there's a fee associated with Junior Day, which usually covers the food and/or a t-shirt provided for that day. However, if the cost is $45 and you don't have the $45, don't let that deter you! You're not obligated to get the meal or t-shirt if applicable. You should be able to opt-out of the lunch and still attend.

However, if you can conjure up the $45 for the lunch, do it! Why? Because sometimes, schools have the lunch hour arranged for student-athletes who play similar positions to eat together at the same table (i.e., running backs table, wide receivers table, linebackers table), and the coaches of those positions will most likely sit with them or visit the table. For the benefit of meeting the coaches and binding with other football moms and their sons, I highly suggest paying the fee. You'll build relationships and gain new contacts.

When you first arrive at Junior Day, you'll typically pay at the door and then receive a questionnaire from the recruiting department for your son to complete. It'll ask him questions like: *How did you get here? Do you live in a two-parent household or a one-parent household? What position do you play? Who is your high school coach? Who is your position coach? What are their phone numbers? What are your social media handles?* The questionnaire gives the university an opportunity to either update their recruiting profile on your son or start the process of getting to know who he is.

Junior Days can be a bit tiring, as it'll usually start around 8 a.m. and last until 4 or 5 that evening; nonetheless, it's imperative to stay all day. Coaches will usually have an area for you to speak to leaders in the compliance department and learn about eligibility. (This will give you an opportunity to reinforce what you're learning in this book, as well.) Even more, you'll receive a true college tour and a meaningful glimpse of the university's culture. A university representative will typically take guests around to the dorms, the library, the academic areas in conjunction with the student-athletes, and highlight other areas on campus. Some universities will have an area set up for exploring multiple degree programs the university offers, where you will also have the chance to ask questions to those who specialize in certain academic departments. Sometimes, coaches will take student-athletes through the college football players' process of getting measured and weighed, as well as putting on the university's jersey and taking pictures. They'll get a tour of the locker room and stadium, as well. Many times, before the day ends, the coaches will even play a very emotional highlight video that captures the essence of their team spirit and accomplishments over the years. It's a rewarding experience you don't want to miss out on.

If you're looking to attend multiple Junior Days, I suggest starting as early as the summer before your son's freshman year, narrowing the list down to three each school year. The reasoning behind this advice is to ensure he has an opportunity to visit the campuses he desires most, in a cost-efficient and smart way.

From afar, it may seem simplistic to go to an endless number of Junior Days the summer before his junior year, but with his high school football demands (as well as any other sports he may be playing), his schoolwork, and the cost of driving or flying to each university, it can become extremely difficult and highly expensive. There are some high-profile student-athletes who will receive almost 50 invites at the start of their junior year. However, there is no need to waste time trying to visit all 50 campuses across the country. Visit the ones that matter most, and do it steadily over the years.

Although coaches may not give a freshman or sophomore as much attention as a junior, due to the NCAA rules, it's still worth the benefits of networking, educating yourself and exposing your son to the world of college campuses early on.

When your son becomes a junior, he won't be allowed to do any "official visits" without first registering and submitting his transcript to the NCAA Eligibility Center (formerly known as the NCAA Clearinghouse). (*We'll talk more about "official visits" in the next section.*) I suggest a student-athlete who is still working on bringing his core GPA up his junior year wait before registering and possibly start his official visits his senior year.

If you are in this predicament, it would make it even more difficult to fit all of his visits into the summer before his senior year. Narrowing down your list now is the smartest way to move forward. Again, set your schedule to visit three universities' Junior Days or unofficial visits each year. Covering the summers before his freshman through senior year, this will make it twelve visits in total. That'll be twelve schools you have built relationships at and gained emails or phone contacts; it'll be four years of hearing expert information about college experiences, college football programs, and the recruiting process.

Another upside to starting your visits early is that once you have exposed your son to multiple college campuses, he'll be over the culture-shock excitement and be able to make decisions that aren't solely based on emotion. (If you are just learning this information and your son is in his sophomore or junior year already, don't worry. Do what you can with the timeframe allowed.) After years of Junior Day visits, you two will both be well-informed, well connected, and able to wisely compare the pros and cons of multiple schools and their offerings.

Official Visits vs. Unofficial Visits

I've mentioned both "official visits" and "unofficial visits" in this book, but I have yet to define the two for you. The difference between an NCAA declared "official visit" and "unofficial visit" is simple to understand. You don't have to pay for "official visits," whereas you are responsible for all expenses of "unofficial visits."

Official visits are paid for by the college, and it includes transportation to and from the college, living arrangements while there, three meals for each day of the visit for the college-bound student-athlete and his parent(s). Official visits cannot extend the length of 48 hours long, or the span of one weekend.

Most official visits, depending on the university, may also include up to three tickets to a home sports game. It's a great deal, but understand that student-athletes are only allotted one expense-paid visit per institution and a maximum of five Division 1 visits in total. However, student-athletes are allowed an unlimited amount of official visits to Division 2 and Division 3 schools.

As mentioned above, before your son can get approved for his official visits starting his junior year, he must register with the NCAA Eligibility Center, submit his academic transcript and be placed on the institutional request list. For Division 1 football programs, student-athletes can start taking official visits April 1 of their junior year through the Sunday before the last Wednesday in June. After the June deadline, he can start taking official visits again beginning the first day of his senior year.

Unofficial visits, on the other hand, give you a lot more freedom. You don't have to go through an approval process by the NCAA, and there's no cap on the number of visits you can have. However, even with all of this wiggle room, it still requires some level of scheduling beforehand. You cannot just show up on campus one day, with no permission from the university, and expect the coaches to be prepared to give the tour and information you're looking for. You must first make proper contact with a staff member in the recruiting department at the university and inquire about scheduling an unofficial visit. (Note that it is illegal for any recruiting coach to pay for anything for you or your student-athlete, whether that be travel expenses or lunch.)

Football Camps

The same way you find out about Junior Days is the same way you can learn about upcoming football camps at different universities. Check online. Colleges will usually have dates on their calendar of events. You can also follow the university on social media platforms because they'll usually post it when the dates are near.

Any student-athlete, freshman through senior year, can attend a camp, and go every year. I suggest going to as many different camps as possible. Your goal is to have his talent displayed and receive an offer, and that will add to his recruitment status.

Tips on choosing the best camps for your child:

- Know your child. If he's ready to play with the big guys, have him participate in a Division 1 camp. If you don't think he's ready for that just yet, it's no problem. Sign him up for a Division 2 or Division 3 camp.
- If your child doesn't run a strong 40, I suggest he doesn't run. The coaches pay close attention to this. You don't want them to write that he's a runner along with a low timed number. It will hurt his recruitment later.
- If your son is injured, don't let him compete at the summer football camps that year. Student-athletes who are very excited to complete may say they can still do it despite the pain, but don't allow it. Let him know that there are camps every year and that next year would be better for him. Trying to play while hurt would only result in him underperforming during the regular season or showing bad results to recruiting coaches.
- Bring your own folding chairs and snacks, and keep a little cooler in the car. You'll be out there for a long time, and it's usually hot! Typically, camps will have two sessions, so you don't want to have to sit on the turf or stand the entire time.

When you're spending time at camps, remember what you learned about networking with coaches in Chapter 4. Your art of approach is everything. You don't want to nag coaches while you attend camps. Enjoy watching your child compete. If coaches are interested in your child, you will know. Someone will make sure you or his high school coach is aware. Remember, as soon as you leave campus, coaches still have to abide by the NCAA rule of not initiating contact with student-athletes who are in their freshman and sophomore years. Your best bet is to gradually build conversational relationships with the coaching staffs you meet at camps, find them on social media platforms, and get their email addresses. Above all else, have fun at the camps! Your son will be enjoying his time meeting new friends, competing, showcasing his skills, and learning what playing for a college team is all about.

7

YOUR SON & SOCIAL MEDIA

THE SPORTS INDUSTRY is shifting. It's not all about athleticism. The attention is now leaning more toward a player's character, and social media has become an undeniable source for learning about one's character and values. People have been known to lose their jobs over inappropriate posts. There's even an NFL coach who lost his entire team behind *one* post. You see, the impact of social media can either be tremendously detrimental or greatly beneficial. The same platform that a student-athlete can promote himself, post his highlights, and get positive exposure, is the same platform that can be his demise.

When you're dealing with the college recruitment process, it's important to know that most universities will conduct "social media evaluations," or social media reports. These evaluations are when a staff member from the football department views all of a player's social media platforms to gain an assessment of the athlete's character. The football staff member observes who the player follows, who and what he's retweeting, what photos or posts he's liking, and more. Everything your son is doing on social media will be being analyzed.

Understand that coaches are looking to weed out anyone who may be a poison to their team. If a student-athlete is using curse words on every other post, it's a red flag. If he's posting photos of himself throwing up his middle finger, wearing his pants sagging, holding a gun, and drinking or smoking at a number of parties, coaches will conclude that this young man is reckless or violent. If he's reposting or retweeting videos of people having sex or fighting, he'll look like someone who's wild or toxic. And that's not the type of student-athlete coaches want to deal with or have influencing other players on their team.

I've seen coaches take their offers back from student-athletes who had inappropriate social media posts. (*Are you seeing just how serious this is?*) Your son, along with everyone else, is judged for what's posted on his social media accounts. There isn't a nicer way to explain it. Whether or not it is unanimous that something your child posts or reposts displays negative characteristics, doesn't matter. At this point, you and your son's attention should be focused on what the coaches will think.

Not only will your son's posts be observed but also the name of his social media handle. His @name shouldn't be anything provocative, drug-related or violent. It's best for him to have a name that's actually his real name across all platforms because he's now creating a brand around himself as a promising player. The good news is that your son is in control of what he posts, so he can ensure he has these things in line and clean.

College coaches are betting great investments on the student-athletes they recruit, and understandably, they are looking to get a return on those investments. They must carefully consider their choices. At the end of the day, coaches only have the freedom to give out 25 scholarships per year. Therefore, if they hand a scholarship to a student-athlete who turns out to be more troublesome than helpful, they lose out on their investment altogether. You see, they don't want to bet their investment on the wrong person.

Recruiting someone who shows signs of poor character early on can easily backfire on them. That same student-athlete may end up getting kicked out of the university years from now because of a behavioral problem. It also backfires as a bad reflection on the coaches and their ability to properly assess young men before recruiting them. This is why coaches will continue to turn to social media to learn more about student-athletes' personal lives in more authentic ways — revealing things that might be withheld during a meeting.

Monitoring Your Son's Social Media

Every household is different. Therefore, I won't say that watching over your son's social media accounts is a mandate, but I will say that it's highly recommended. In order to help lead your son in the right direction for his future in sports, it is so important that you are fully aware of what he is posting and re-sharing on his pages.

If you have a close-knit relationship with your son, this will probably be easy to accomplish. He may not have an issue with you having his login information, seeing his posts, and asking him to take certain things down that you don't approve of. On the other hand, if your son has you manually blocked from seeing his pages or you know it will start issues between you two if you ask about it, there are ways to still get what you need. Consider creating a secret, dummy page to follow him, and then, you can view his posts in private. If you're a parent who feels you are wrongfully invading your son's privacy if you sign into his account, I suggest that you also create a secret, dummy page to view his posts in private. You don't need to make unnecessary problems in your home, but you *do* need to stay aware!

In the process of monitoring his social media pages, whether you're doing it in privately or openly, be prepared to deal with it if you notice he is posting or re-sharing things that you know will hurt his image in the long run. You will have to sit him down and have a conversation about his future.

While doing this, be sure he understands the importance of upholding a positive image on social media and remind him of this often. Be adamant about it. If he doesn't listen to you, play defense. Screenshot the inappropriate posts and send them to his high school coach, asking him to speak to your son about the importance of his image. Many coaches would be willing to help with this, especially if the mom has already tried getting through to her child.

At the end of the day, any student-athlete who is

serious about being recruited to play college football and wants a possible future in the NFL will *have to* adhere to this advice.

8

HELPING THE SUFFERING ATHLETE

THE "GET YOUR act together" response to an athlete who is suffering emotionally, mentally, or athletically will not work. Suffering student-athletes are usually secretly dealing with internal struggles, such as stress, depression, sadness, anger or confusion, and in turn, they need special attention given to their issues in order to recover to a healthier state. It's an issue that must never be ignored.

As we all know, athletes are often told to *suck it up*, and because of that, they struggle to communicate their emotions or frustrations. Many don't know how to respond to what they're dealing with outside of what they've been taught, so these issues tend to fester into larger problems in their lives. As a parent, you must be aware of the signs of your student-athlete suffering.

Red Flags

One of the main indicators of a suffering athlete is a change in behavior. If you notice a student-athlete who is normally well-behaved start to act out of character, it's a red flag that he's most likely suffering from an emotional or psychological issue. His behavior is a sign that those closest to him must intentionally pay attention to and not brush off by saying, "Get your act together."

If he is lashing out, slamming doors, cursing more than usual, terribly slacking in his grades, using drugs, turning to violence, or engaging in any other disruptive behaviors, it's time to trace back to where this problem is coming from and get help. His changes could have sprouted from a number of things, such as his family not having enough money, experiencing pain from the absence of his father, witnessing violence in his household, dealing with his parents' separation or divorce, feeling pressures on and off the field, extreme stress, or even feeling inadequate in certain areas. The list goes on. Although most won't be vocal about their circumstances, it's still imperative to take every red flag seriously — immediately.

Despite a young man's background or family environment, pain is pain and stress is stress. It can happen to any one of them. While helping suffering athletes, I've witnessed some stories that have brought me to tears. It's both encouraging and heartbreaking to hear young men open up about things they've suffered from so long in silence.

I remember dealing with a college athlete who started regularly smoking weed; something he'd never done before. After asking the right questions to get to his reasoning behind this change, we learned that it wasn't the peer pressure or an identity crisis but the extreme stress he was under that pushed him to do it. He knew smoking weed, or smoking anything for that matter, would negatively affect his future and possibly lead to a suspension, but he was willing to sacrifice that for what seemed to be peace of mind through getting high. Trying to juggle schoolwork, football, training, and free-time with friends among many other demands surrounding them is undoubtedly difficult for any teenager.

Moms must also consider if they are exhibiting any red flags of their own that could have a negative effect on their child. Constantly saying phrases like, "My son is going to the NFL, and he's going to take care of his mother," can add unnecessary weight on your son's shoulders as well. Although it is great for him to make it to the NFL and take care of his family, there needs to be a level of balance here. Pushing him in one direction and telling him that he's responsible for pulling the entire family out of poverty or middle-class status is not healthy. It's actually damaging. It can cause your son to resent you in the future, especially if this is something *you want* more than he does. Therefore, any glimpse of your son negatively responding to such comments, I suggest you take a step back. Ask him how he feels about you making those comments. Ask him about his passions outside of football, too. You don't want him to think his life is football or nothing! If that's the case, he will suffer through every failure that comes along through his football career.

There have to be balanced options presented to your son so he can live a healthy, happy life and not a mentally stressed or depressed life. He must know that he has a brilliant brain that can do more than strategize how to make touchdowns. Therefore, if you notice even a hint of a red flag exposing that he may be suffering from this type of pressure, sit him down and open his eyes to limitless possibilities. Show him that he has the ability to apply the same energy he puts toward the game of football to anything else he wants to accomplish. The key here is to discern if your son is suffering from the pressure of your (or anyone else's) high standards for his football career. The goal is for him to be excited about his future, not stressed out about it.

Over 80 percent of the student-athletes I've worked with in the past have had issues that led back to being over-stressed. There are so many people telling them what to do and what they *can* become if they do what they say that the overload comes down on them all at once. If student-athletes don't get the help they need to overcome psychological issues and stress, it can put limits on what they achieve in the future. And that's definitely not what we want. It's best to buckle them down now and teach them how to positively channel those frustrations into their ambitions, athleticism, and out on the field.

Seeking Help

Whether your son is suffering emotionally, mentally, academically or athletically there is always a place to find help. For those dealing with a psychological issue or extreme stress, I suggest bringing him to a therapist. (*Before you dismiss this option, moms, hear me out.*) If you've never had a therapist, you might not understand the benefits of seeing one. It's like having a best friend without the possibility of backlash or backstabbing. They listen to you spill your deepest secrets and emotions without judging you, and they give you the comfort of confidentiality to never share it with anyone else. It offers a level of relief that doesn't compare to anything else. Getting all of your feelings out there on the table, with nothing held back, is therapeutic and can create a tremendous breakthrough for someone who is dealing with psychological issues or stress — especially a student-athlete. High school students may also have on-campus counselors or social workers they can look to for help.

If your son is a Christian, you can reach out to a spiritual support group. Building a closer relationship with God and Christ (for those who believe in Christianity) can bring a stressed or emotionally distressed person into a healthy recovery. The worry, anxiety, or damaging thoughts can be wiped away when a child realizes the truth of who they are in Christ and the power they have to overcome such mental or emotional turmoil.

I also suggest checking out your son's friends and his usual surroundings. Having the right friends and accountability partners around have proven to make a world of difference in people's lives. Some are simply dealing with not having anyone to turn to who can lead them through a bad day — someone they can lean on when things get tough. Now, mom, that accountability partner might not be you, as much as you would like it to be. Know your son, and if he's more comfortable talking to someone else about his problems, guide him in learning to turn to that person as a supporter, mentor or accountability partner.

Let's say your son is suffering in other areas, such as academics or athletics, there are resources you can find to help him gain the skills or knowledge he needs to improve in those areas as well. If he is struggling academically, you can search for tutors, as I've mentioned in earlier chapters. If the school doesn't provide access to tutors, there will usually be tutors in the community who offer professional services.

To help him even further, ask his teachers if he can possibly do extra work to bring his grades up, and she might be able to help him out. Athletically, you can find an outside trainer who is good in football to help your son improve his techniques, or you can partner him with a skilled mentor or high school coach who doesn't mind walking him through the areas he's struggling with on the field.

If your son is suffering in any area, it's imperative for you to address the red flags you notice, ask questions, allow him the space to be vulnerable, and seek help. Ignoring the quiet pains of a suffering athlete can cost him his entire future, so you want to ensure you are fully tending to his needs through to recovery.

9

CHOOSING THE RIGHT COLLEGE

MUCH LIKE CHOOSING the right high school, choosing the right college entails the importance of understanding the school's culture, the coach's personality, the team structure, the challenges of transition, and the issues of drugs and peer pressure that may occur.

However, to choose the right college you will have to take into account more than you did when you were choosing a high school. Your son will be away from home, living independently, and still required to be responsible and make the best decisions for his adult life. The college he attends will have a lot to do with how he matures and the outcome of his future.

The Transition

I've witnessed a number of student-athletes get offered to a college and then attend their first year believing they are about to outshine everyone on the team. Sadly, this mindset usually leaves them disappointed.

Although a student-athlete may have been a star on his high school football team, he must realize that he's jumping into an entirely different pool. His collegiate team will most likely have a slew of other high-caliber players. He'll be playing with those who can match him in size, speed, and skill. Therefore, ensure your son comes into this new transition and experience being realistic, humble, and ready to learn.

The Roster

If you are not a football guru, have an unbiased person look at the roster of your son's top college choices. Have them break it down and explain the different techniques and style of play of each university. With this information, you'll know which schools are best for your son.

When observing the style of college teams, you also want to take into account the size of the players that the coaches seem to favor in recruiting. If a school has a team made of majority six foot and taller players but your son is much shorter and still received an offer, you may want to reconsider committing to this school. Why? Because the coach may just be filling a spot he's having trouble recruiting for, although he's not totally sold on your son's size. In other words, your son isn't his "type," but he's taking him to keep a scholarship from going to waste, or for other unknown reasons. This can become a serious issue down the road. When other players who *are* the coach's type join the team, the coach will gravitate toward them when organizing play time on the field.

Sure, it's a natural instinct for coaches to gravitate toward their preference in a player's build, but you will not want your son in this position. In most cases, he'll likely get seldom time on the field to play simply because he is not the coach's "type." Noticing this early on can help protect your son.

Keep in mind, no coach is the same. I've witnessed coaches play student-athletes who were not their "type" but too talented to ignore. Although you may cross coaches who are stuck in their ways and turn away from players who don't fit their mold, there are other coaches who don't have a type, at all. In the end, it will be you and your son's responsibility to recognize where he fits best. The goal is to ensure he is recruited to a team that celebrates him and not tolerates him.

A New Living Environment

Now, let's talk about the school's culture and the city's atmosphere. He'll be living in a new environment for a few years. If he commits to an out-of-state college, you'll have more things to consider, as this will be a drastic transition to grow accustomed to. For instance, what does the food taste like? Are his favorite things to eat and do available in this new place? Can he bear the weather? Is there an airport in this city? If not, how far away is it? How much would it cost to book a flight and hotel room near him? How long is the drive from where you live now?

As simple as that may seem, it's important to consider the smallest details when making a move. Majority of students who leave for college go through mild depression. They become homesick and yearn to get back to their old lives and the things they are used to.

Peer Pressure & Drugs

The level of peer pressure and its effects on student-athletes in college would stupefy you. In college, student-athletes are exposed to drugs, threesomes, performance enhancers, one-night stands, a lot of unprotected sex, drug dealers, unethical agents willing to give them money, runners willing to give them whatever they ask for, rejection, desire to stay fashionable, girls who are trying to pick up a potential NFL player, shared pills, attention, weed, cocaine and other addictive drugs, abusive relationships, disconnections with coaches, anxiety, excessive alcohol drinking, pressure to give elite performances on the field, and more other psychological stressors. The list goes on.

Some moments of pressure may occur at times you least expect. For instance, student-athletes are required to dress up on games days, and for some student-athletes, this invites another phase of peer pressure. If he doesn't own the proper business attire or doesn't have the money to buy the expensive clothes his peers are wearing for every football game, he can easily become embarrassed, angry, or even worse, teased. I've watched some students stress out because their teammates were looking as if they walked out of a GQ magazine. They felt the pressure to dress just as well as the others, but because they couldn't afford to, it created a sense of inadequacy.

When it comes to the severity of drugs and the pressures that come along with that, my best advice to you is to familiarize both yourself and your son with the drug policies and programs of each university you are considering. The drug policies and programs vary by university, and you don't want to assume you'll never need assistance in this area. In all honesty, most parents are naive in thinking that their son would never do drugs. They find themselves disappointed in a lot of cases. The most commonly used drug to be aware of is marijuana. Marijuana has derailed more student-athletes' opportunities than I can count.

One of the first things that a university conducts upon arrival, amongst other tests, will be a drug test. In most cases, if a student-athlete fails a drug test upon arrival, he will be placed into the university's drug program. With a disciplinary action in place, drug use can postpone a student-athlete from touching the field. It can also cause a student-athlete to be totally suspended from competing in this NCAA sport and get him kicked out of the university altogether. In an event where an athlete who uses is still lucky enough to make it to the NFL, this issue can cost him a lot of money! Whether you believe your son will fall into this circle of drug use or not, it is definitely a possibility you must come to recognize and look out for early on.

Think about all of the peer pressures you had to endure when you were around your son's age. Now, magnify that by a thousand. The pressure will be high and tempting for your son to lose himself in the uproar. This is why the college you choose is important. The culture, environment, and policies in place can make a great difference. There may even be red flags you or your son encounter while visiting different campuses. Be sure to have an adult conversation with him about the things he may experience in college and guide him in making the wisest choice when it's time to commit to a school.

Degree Programs & Athlete Support

Parents must also consider the degree programs certain colleges offer. Not all schools offer the same areas of study. Although he'll be playing football, we know that not everyone will be drafted into the NFL. He'll need a solid backup plan. The best way to prepare is to ensure the school offers the degree he is seriously interested in pursuing for a career. I worked with a student-athlete in the past who was interested in videography, so he committed to a college that offered a video production program. The other schools who sent him offers didn't have this program, so for him, the decision was easy. Your son should follow suit when making his ultimate decision of commitment.

Beyond exploring the degree programs offered, you'll also want to ask the right questions about the athletic department's academic support system and educational tools available. I know of a school's athletic department that spends nearly a quarter of a million dollars each year on their educational support for athletes; they even give each athlete a personal tutor. It's just that important to them. While at another school, this may not be the case. They may have five players sharing one tutor, or worse, a couple tutors for the entire team.

Let's say your son is coming from a high school that doesn't have the best educational background. Well, when he enters the collegiate realm, it'll take a lot more effort to keep his grades up. He won't be able to miss class or extra study time with a tutor. As an active parent, you will also want to be in contact with his academic advisor and know what GPA he needs to maintain to ensure he doesn't lose eligibility to play on the team or lose his good standing at the university.

Although attending class is usually mandatory for student-athletes, some athletic leaders fail to ensure their players are actually passing in their classes. If your son is known to slack on his work, not only will you need to ensure the football team has an academic support system in place that can help him when he needs it most but also a staff that is strict about their athletes being in every class. The college world is all about independence, so no one will be holding his hand. However, having an athletic department that's strict on academics will at least push him to make the right decisions if he truly cares about securing his future on the team.

From a medical standpoint on support, you'll want to ask questions about their health assistance. How many doctors and athletic trainers does the team have on staff? Do the players have access to nutritionists or healthy eating plans? What is the protocol when an athlete gets injured during practice or a game? Do parents have access to their son's medical records if anything happens to him? Ensuring you will have the right access, contacts, and support is key when deciding on the best college for your son.

College Schedule

College schedules are the real deal! Prepare your son for what he'll be getting himself into. Student-athletes in college rarely have a life outside of football and schoolwork. For example, here is what a typical football player's schedule will look like:

- 6:00 a.m. – 6:30 a.m. | Wake up
- 7:00 a.m. – 8:00 a.m. | Breakfast Club (An Early Study Hall)
- 9:00 a.m. – 1:00 p.m.| Class
- [Quick Break]
- 2:15 p.m. – 6:30 p.m. | Football Practices and Meetings
- 7:00 p.m. – 9:00 p.m. | Late Study Hall

The best advice for navigating such a strict and busy schedule is to remember what the main goal is at the end of the day. Your son will be at a college he worked very hard to reach and on the road to achieving greater things in his life. Remind him that this is a season of focus and to diligently stay the course. Hard work always pays off.

Money Management

Another area you should learn about during this process is your son's pay. How much will he get paid? How often does he receive the money? College athletes will usually get a monthly payment to assist with expenses throughout the school year.

At Division 1 schools, in some cases, student-athletes will get around $1,200 or more a month, as well as a recurring Pell Grant, which can sometimes be around $4,000 each school year, through Federal Student Aid. That's a lot of money for an eighteen-year-old to handle. If you can keep up with how much and how often he gets paid (*without being controlling, of course*), I suggest doing it.

Monitor how he manages his finances, and if he needs your help, step in and show him ways he can make wiser spending decisions.

The Athlete-Coach Relationship

The relationship between an athlete and a coach is just like any other relationship — it will survive only through compatibility. The two must have thoughts, feelings, and behaviors that work well together. You must understand that your son's performance, skills, and athleticism, especially on the collegiate level, will thrive best when he's partnered with a coach who meshes well with him and doesn't create extreme conflict.

As you begin to communicate with recruiting coaches, pay attention to what they will and won't tolerate in behavior. If the coach has zero tolerance for players who are flip, quickly angered, or don't have a filter when speaking and your son falls into one of these categories, make sure he thinks twice before committing to this school. It doesn't matter how anxious you are to have your son go to a certain school; if he's flip and the coach will not tolerate it, the two of them will not get along.

If you speak with a different type of coach, one who has the patience to deal with players who are flip or struggle with anger problems, then your son will have a better chance at soaring on this coach's team. You see, these are the things you want to look out for ahead of time in order to find a place where your son can become his best self.

You also want to consider your son's experience with a college football playbook and the coach's willingness to teach him how to read it. One of the main reasons players don't have a chance to play on the field in their early years of college is because they struggle with the playbook; they don't under-stand it and are too embarrassed to ask for help.

If you know your son doesn't understand X's and O's, you may want to look for a situation where the coaches are open to teaching new players one-on-one how to read it.

Unlike high school, your son's football career will be on the line like never before. You don't want his relationship with his coach to be the thing clouding his opportunity or holding him back. Overall, you and your son must define the standard of what it is you want and don't want for his college football experience and then choose accordingly.

10

DEAR MOMS

MOMS, YOU ARE superheroes. The fact that you grabbed this book and read it to the very last chapter proves that you are ready and willing to take on the challenges that come along with college football recruitment and eligibility and with having a son who's an athlete. It also shows that you aren't afraid of the lengthy process that comes along with educating yourself and ensuring your son reaches his full potential.

Despite your heroism, you may still feel as if you are a worried mom, a nonchalant mom, a financially struggling mom, or an unfulfilled mom who needs encouragement to keep going. Well, this chapter is here to speak to and inspire you in each of those areas. But, before we get into that, there are a few things I'd like you to remember on this journey through college football recruitment and eligibility.

Remember to think of football recruiting like dating. When you first meet a man, there is always a lot of fluffiness, a lot of wining and dining going on. The same goes for football recruiting. In the beginning, coaches are trying to woo you and your son; they are saying all the right things to make you comfortable, and they're leaving out all of the bad stuff to keep you close. Therefore, in order to make the best choice, you must look beyond the fluff. For instance, a coach can say your son can be on the starting lineup his freshman year, but that's vague. You have to be realistic about the depth chart. See where your son falls on the list and the likelihood of him actually playing his freshman year.

As we've discussed before, coaches are under a lot of pressure to choose the best athletes during recruitment. Their jobs are on the line, so I'm not saying their wooing is to be looked down upon. However, you have to use discernment to make an educated decision that's best for *your* family. As stated in Chapter 9, you and your son must consider the little things about a school, like the culture of the city, the food, the distance from home, the cost of travel, and other aspects that are tailored to your specific needs and desires.

In addition, know when a coach is not interested; it's similar to when a man isn't interested in dating. Trust me, if he's not blowing up your phone or answering your calls, he's probably not interested in recruiting your son. He probably has another student-athlete on his mind. His backing away is your cue to move on to a different offer. Your son can go where he's appreciated or try to get a spot where he's only tolerated. And like all moms, you will want your son to be on a team where he's fully appreciated, so make your decision accordingly.

Remember that it's a myth that your son has to go to a big university in order to get drafted into the NFL. That's not true at all. Scouts will look under every rock to find talent, so if your son is good, they will come and get him! A bigger college may perhaps give your son a bigger platform, but that doesn't mean a small college can keep him from reaching the next level. If he has next-level talent, he will make it.

Remember to take time to discover your son's passions and figure out what he wants to study for his degree prior to committing to a college for football. If football doesn't work out, you want to ensure he's not stuck with an irrational degree focus, like general studies. It's best to settle on a major he's truly interested in studying for an industry he'd like to have a career in one day.

Last but not least, remember to never allow a

coach or anyone else to put extreme pressure on you or your son during this time of recruitment. By no means will this process be easy, but you can definitely control the level of stress you allow to weigh you and your son.

―――――――

The Worried Mom

As a parent, I know you want the very best for your child. It's understandable. Many mothers worry about their sons making the right decision, making it through recruitment, being safe in a different environment or state, having an injury when they're not around, needing extra money or food to live comfortably on campus, being around the wrong influences, not choosing the best academic program to study, and so on. Some also worry about having to miss their sons' games if they are recruited far out of state. Of course, your mind may wander to some of the worst possible scenarios, but as your son goes through the recruitment process and then leaves for college, you cannot have worry constantly consuming your day.

If you don't begin to settle your thoughts on this

issue, the stress can take an emotional toll on your life and possibly even turn into a medical condition. I know of a football mom who suffered from a heart attack when her son was maneuvering through the recruitment process and dealing with the demands of different coaches and colleges. Learn from this worried mother's mistake of over-stressing, and be adamant about finding ways to relieve the pressure early on.

Here are three things I suggest you do to help eliminate any stress or worry:

- When a coach begins pursuing your son, be sure to ask if he is the position coach who your son will be working with after recruitment. What most parents don't understand is that many times the coach recruiting their son is not the coach who will be working hand-in-hand with him throughout his college football career. You don't want to be blindsided when you start communicating with the recruiting coach and expect him to be the one you will be communicating with thereafter. You should build a relationship with his position coach — the one who will be personally coaching your son, the one who you know will have him in arms reach.
- Collegiate teams will have a Director of

Player Personnel, a man or woman on staff who manages the players' recruitment and players' support. You will want to build a relationship with this person as well. Coaches turn to the Player Personnel when they need to deal with a student in any way. Therefore, you can count on this person to have inside intel on your son while he's on the team. If you build a close enough relationship with him or her, you may receive courtesy calls to keep you in the loop of what's going on with your son. For instance, if your son is dealing with anger issues, the Player Personnel's recruiting and support team will be the ones to ensure he finds help to get his anger issues under control. Remember that during football season it can be nearly impossible to reach a coach, so having close contact with the support team can come in handy when you have questions. Another thing I don't want to leave out here: refrain from being a complex, overpowering, difficult mom for the staff to deal with. Reach out with a friendly attitude, sweet holiday cards, and only occasional calls of serious concerns.

- For moms who have sons moving out of state, be sure to look for a school with a family environment of coaches. With a close-knit, homelike atmosphere on campus, you can rest assured that he'll be well taken care of while you're not there.

The Nonchalant Mom

A mom who doesn't understand the gravity of her son's talent or potential will move around carelessly. She will indirectly affect her son in a negative way and add to his psychological stressors. If she doesn't start to tend to his future and educate herself to feed his mind and ears with the right information, her son can become susceptible to anything life throws his way.

You see, being nonchalant is not acceptable anymore. As a parent, you are your son's protection, and when that coverage isn't there, it shows — and it hurts. What I've come to learn is that when some coaches don't think a student-athlete has a strong support system, they treat him in a way that reflects that. (*Not all coaches, but some.*) They have more respect for those with backing — with a mom who will step in and speak up when necessary.

During recruitment, most student-athletes are simply innocents in the mix of things, and they don't fully recognize maliciousness in the adults around. They miss the red flags from someone who is trying to get over on them or lie to win them over. The truth is that this recruitment process can be heartless and cruel, and without the protection of caring parents and guardians, our young men suffer.

I've seen moms who didn't care much in the beginning cry in the end. Why? Because they wished they had educated themselves properly, taken their sons potential seriously, and protected him through the process. It's imperative that parents don't slack or wait to learn as much as they can about this industry for their child.

If you know of other football moms, especially those who seem to be nonchalant when it comes to the sports part of their sons' lives, give them a copy of this book or tell them about it. Whether our children are five or ten years old, we have to start encouraging each other to reach for the stars, as well as educating our student-athletes and guiding them to success.

The Financially Struggling Mom

I've met some amazing women who have done the impossible to make sure their children thrive in their skills and talents. I've even met mothers who made less than $20,000 a year but managed to raise four children off of that. Not to mention, they were able to make do for their student-athletes. I've seen single mothers do some amazing things with little money, and now looking back at what my mom used to do for me as a single parent, I am astonished and inspired. It proves that you can do this! Despite what financial state you're in, you have the ability to not only manage it but also advance yourself in many ways.

Whether you are making minimum wage, didn't get a college education, or feel you are being treated and paid inadequately at your job, you don't have to settle for those unfavorable circumstances. Stop asking yourself: *Why me? Why my family?* Instead, ask: *How can I take what I have and advance myself and my family? How can I challenge myself the way I am pushing my son to challenge himself in the classroom and on the field?* Those who feel trapped in financial struggles, start setting financial goals for yourself. (Keep referring back to Chapter 3, where I focus on what goes into investing in your child and give tips for saving and raising money.)

What you want to make sure you avoid is putting all the pressure on your son to take care of the family one day. In Chapter 8, I covered how this unnecessary weight on your son's shoulders can cause him to suffer. Many financially struggling families believe that once a student-athlete is drafted into the NFL they will be automatically taken out of poverty, and that's not the case. Most of the guys who make it there take home thousands but not millions, as many assume. Therefore, they are not in a position to immediately take their entire family out of poverty.

There was one woman I worked with in the past who thought her son would be bringing home a lot more money, but he wasn't a high draft pick. You see, high draft picks are drafted in early rounds, whereas other athletes are drafted in later rounds, which result in a lot less money. She was disheartened to find out their financial situation wasn't going to be drastically changed.

This is why I want financially struggling mothers to challenge themselves to grow in this area and look at what they *do* have, without having to wait to see what their son could possibly bring home one day. Let's say hypothetically, you get $7,000 back from your income tax refund each year. You can put aside $2,000 to help with immediate bills, $2,000 to help with your student-athlete's current and future expenses, and then save $3,000 toward building your own dreams. After 5 years, you can have $15,000 saved to start buying property, purchasing things for a business idea you have, or buying collateral to offset your life. You'll also have $10,000 aside to help with your son's football expenses.

In all honesty, whether you are impoverished, working paycheck to paycheck, or well-off, being able to travel to see your son play at an out-of-state or distant college every weekend is expensive. As I also mentioned in Chapter 3, you'll need money saved to get a hotel, food, and a plane ticket, which might cost up to a $1,000 or more a weekend. Listen, if you have to drive for Lyft to make an extra $1,000 a month, do it! You may lose some free time and might not be able to go out with your friends every weekend, but it will be a worthy sacrifice.

Despite where you are now, whether you're working at a fast food restaurant or a teacher, see what your potential really is. You can reach every goal you set. Think of yourself in a better light and let nothing discourage you from living the life you desire.

The Unfulfilled Mom

Here's a tough question for most football moms to answer: *Is your son your life?* Much like a financially struggling mom, an unfulfilled mom tends to put an overload of pressure on her son to get a college offer and "make it" to the NFL because she has no ambitions outside of him. Then, when he goes off to college, she feels lost, as if there is nothing left for her to do. All of her dreams are tightly wrapped up in caring for her son's needs, and without him around, she feels unfulfilled.

This is not a strange feeling for a mother who has centered her entire life around her son's and has to face the fact that he's no longer in the house, she's not bringing him to and from football practice every other day, the recruiting process is over, and her Friday nights are now quite open. It's a tough transition, but it's not impossible to survive.

Mothers, the best thing you can do is catch yourself from falling into this bubble of feeling unfulfilled early. Begin simultaneously focusing on your dreams as you focus on your son's future. If you want to go back to college, don't hesitate to make it happen. We are in 2018, and there are 50 and 60-year-olds who are going back to college, starting new careers, and building new businesses. There is no excuse. You can pursue an online program if you have to. I'm not trying to make it seem simplistic by any means. I know getting things in order to go back to college or start a business is not easy, but there is a wide range of resources you can access for assistance with this.

Believe in yourself. Again, see yourself in a different light. Although I see mothers as superheroes, I find that many don't view themselves that way.

Instead, they beat themselves up about what they *should've* done or *can't* do now. It's time you start looking beyond the circumstances and beyond your educational status and reminding yourself of who you truly are, what you are capable of achieving, and what you can add to this world and your family's legacy.

I have a sister who never graduated from high school and ended up having five children while she was still pretty young. Although she was busy with the demands of raising her children, hair and nails were the two things she found joy in finding extra time to do. And the best part was that she was really skilled in doing it. So, I pushed her. I encouraged her to go to school for hair and nails and become a professional. I'd witnessed many professionals in that field make tons of money, and I was confident that she was able to change her life around with it. All she had to do was believe in herself, and when she did, she finally started making a difference in her life and fulfilling her dreams.

Whatever it is that you love to do, whether that be baking, cooking, doing hair, doing nails, communicating with people, interior designing, painting, teaching or whatever, go for it. Stop focusing on social media so much and being led to believe that success happens overnight because it doesn't. It might take you five to seven years to get where you want to be, but at least you'll get there and no longer live below your means.

I remember working with a mother whose inner-dialogue was planted in the idea of her son "making it." *When my son makes it to the NFL, I'm going to do this,* she'd say. *I'm going to do that.* However, as the years went on, her son's chances of making it to the NFL didn't look well. One day, she and I were talking over the phone about it and I asked her a tough question, one that would help her see the truth of the matter.

"What are you going to do if your son doesn't make it?" I asked.

"You know what?" she paused. "I never thought about that."

"Well, you need to think about that," I replied. "You have three other children you have to raise. Building your life around the contingency of this son's actions may not turn out in your favor."

A couple weeks later, we talked again, and this time, she said, "I want you to know that I've enrolled in school."

I was so proud of her. She had finally realized that waiting on her son to "make it" before she got her life together wasn't the best way to live. It made my heart smile. She saw what she was capable of and her fulfillment was no longer all about her son. To get here, all she needed was someone to challenge her with the right questions, like, *What if your son doesn't make it? What's the game plan then? Where will your life stand?* That little push helped her to start putting things in place for her own future, and it also kept her away from putting her son into a box labeled *Football or Nothing*, in order to feel financially safe.

Find out what it is that you love to do and chase that dream! Living with purpose is the key to being fulfilled—in a way that doesn't cause for you to live through your son's life.

I can't say this enough: don't instill in your child's mind that he is only a football player. Add to it. Broaden it. There is no longevity in this sport. No matter how talented a player is, the sport comes with an expiration date. As much as they love football, football does not love them back. It's a temporary experience, and you cannot fully set your child up for success when you are only instilling in him what's temporary. Even if he makes it to the NFL, he should know that he's more than a good player. As I mentioned in Chapter 8, there has to be a balance of options for him early on. He has to know that he can be a football player and an entrepreneur. That once he retires from football, he can be a future doctor, photographer, barber, broadcaster, politician, author, filmmaker, engineer, or any other career he wants to pursue. As you begin embarking on your identity and dreams, be sure to encourage him on his own journey to finding his identity out-side of the sport. As you advance and expand, so will he.

To All Moms

Your son is more than an athlete, as you are more than a football mom. You are a legacy-builder. You have the power to break generational curses, guide your family into a life they have always dreamed of, achieve your ceiling-shattering goals, and make a difference in this world for years to come. You are sure to be an inspiration to your son, a role model for other football moms, and a true light in this sports industry.

A SIMPLE GUIDE FOR NAVIGATING NCAA.ORG

1. First, find the *About Us* tab in the top menu of ncaa.org and explore the subpages listed.

   - On the *What is the NCAA?* page, you will learn what the NCAA organization is dedicated to, as well as their beliefs, values, and commitments. *On Our Three Divisions* page, you will learn the difference between Division 1, Division 2, and Division 3 and how they operate.
   - The *Academics* page may be one of the most important pages you'll visit. Here, you will learn about the opportunities the NCAA provides to help student-athletes learn, compete, and grow off the field.

Other pages you should explore under the *About Us* tab include the following: *Well-being*, *Fairness*, and *Resources*.

2. Next, find the *Student-Athletes* tab in the top menu and follow the subsections titled *Future* and *Current*. Read through the pages listed, which include the following: *Want to Play College Sports?*, *The Value of College Sports*, *National Letter of Intent*, *NCAA Eligibility Center*, *Want to Transfer?*, and *Leadership Development Programs and Resources* sections.

   - On the *NCAA Eligibility Center page*, follow through with registering your student-athlete in the system.
   - To stay updated on what's going on with college eligibility, be sure to also follow the NCAA Eligibility Center Twitter account, @ncaaec.
   - Toward the bottom of the *NCAA Eligibility Center* page, there is a contact section, which lists a toll-free hotline number (877-622-2321) for parents and student-athletes to call for ques-

tions and more information.

- ○ Under each Division tab in the top menu, you'll find pages for *Academics, Compliance, Governance, Recruiting, NCAA Online Directory* and more. Take time on each of those pages.
- ○ The *NCAA Online Directory* page is where you will find the athletic contact information for all universities. In the area provided, type in the name of the university your son is interested in attending, and it will reveal a contact list of coaches. Once you learn a coach's name, it is smart to Google him. Learn as much as you can about your son's potential coach. If you stumble upon his social media account, follow him.

3. Finally, scroll down to the footer of the NCAA website where you'll discover a link to the *FAQs*, where some of the most important questions parents have are answered. There are multiple questions that pertain to academic requirements and recruiting regulations. Spend time reading through the answers to properly educate

yourself in those areas.

HIGH SCHOOL
YEAR-BY-YEAR
CHECKLIST

FRESHMAN YEAR

Summer Before Freshman Year

- __ Meet with your student-athlete's counselor.
- __ Review his 4-year plan to determine how many core classes he will take between his freshman and junior year.
- __ Find small football camps for your son to attend in order to familiarize him (and yourself) with football camps.
- __ Attempt to place your son in "core" electives (or classes that are fun but still classify as NCAA core courses). See the school's counselor or view the high school's 48-H (known as the list of NCAA approved core courses) yourself. (See Chapter 2.)

Freshman Year

- __ Schedule a meeting with your son's new

teachers.

- __ Identify 2-5 colleges to visit for Junior Days, unofficial visits and camps during the upcoming summer. Visit each of the prospect colleges' websites to obtain dates of upcoming camps.
- __ Create your summer calendar!
- __ Consider gifting your son's teachers with something thoughtful for Teacher Appreciation Day. This special day will normally fall on a Tuesday during the National Teacher Appreciation Week, which is the first full week of May.
- __ Start saving money if you haven't already for the summer session.
- __ Ensure your son has a regular medical check-up. Stay on top of getting him medical treatment if he experiences any injuries, big or small.
- __ Review his progress reports to determine if you need to schedule a meeting with his teachers/counselors.
- __ By the end of this year, your son should've taken at least 4-6 core courses:
    - __ 1 English class
    - __ 1 math class
    - __ 1 social studies class
    - __ 1 social science class

- ○   __ 1 comparative religion or foreign language class

SOPHOMORE YEAR

Summer Before Sophomore Year

- __ If your son's final report included a D or F in any class, enroll him in summer school, if available. If he doesn't have any D's or F's but he has over four C's in core classes, have him enroll in at least one summer core class to help push the C to a B. (Remember, C's shouldn't be the objective.) If your son has all C's in his core classes he will yield a 2.0 core GPA.
- __ Attend scheduled Junior Days, unofficial visits, and camps.
- __ Have your son create a Top College Choices list of ten schools he's interested in committing to.
- __ Consider signing your son up for a 7-on-7 team. This can help him gain additional exposure and experience.
- __ Ensure your son has a regular medical

check-up. Stay on top of getting him medical treatment if he experiences any injuries, big or small.

Sophomore Year

- __ Schedule a meeting with your son's new teachers.
- __ Start taking ACT prep-classes.
- __ Identify 2-5 colleges to visit for Junior Days, unofficial visits and camps during the upcoming summer. Visit each of the prospect colleges' websites to obtain dates of upcoming camps.
- __ Create your summer calendar!
- __ Consider gifting your son's teachers with something thoughtful for Teacher Appreciation Day. This special day will normally fall on a Tuesday during the National Teacher Appreciation Week, which is the first full week of May.
- __ Start saving money if you haven't already for the summer session.
- __ Ensure your son has a regular medical check-up. Stay on top of getting him medical treatment if he experiences any injuries, big or small.

- __ Review his progress reports to determine if you need to schedule a meeting with his teachers/counselors.
- __ By the end of this year, your son should've taken at least 4-6 core courses:
  - __ 1 English class
  - __ 1 math class
  - __ 1 social studies class
  - __ 1 social science class
  - __ 1 comparative religion or foreign language class

JUNIOR YEAR

Summer Before Junior Year

- __ If your son's final report included a D or F in any class, enroll him in summer school, if available. If he doesn't have any D's or F's but he has over four C's in core classes, have him enroll in at least one summer core class to help push the C to a B. (Remember, C's shouldn't be the objective.) If your son has all C's in his core classes he will yield a 2.0 core GPA.

- __ Have your son narrow his Top College Choices list down to five schools that he's interested in committing to.

- __ Attend scheduled Junior Days, unofficial visits, and camps. (The summer calendar you prepared for this month may have shifted depending on the number of Junior Day invites he may have received throughout the year.)

- __ Continue with 7-on-7 team efforts if it's helping with his exposure and experience.

- __ Ensure your son has a regular medical check-up. Stay on top of getting him medical treatment if he experiences any injuries, big or small.

Junior Year

- __ Schedule a meeting with your son's new teachers.

- __ Use your son's Top College Choices list to identify the 5 colleges he would like to attend and visit for his NCAA approved "official visits." (Remember, official visits are mutually agreed upon between the student-athlete and the college of interest. Your son must first register with the NCAA Eligibility Center (formerly known as the NCAA Clearinghouse) at eligibility-center.org, submit his academic transcript and be placed on the institutional request list. Remember, a student-athlete can start taking official visits by April 1st of his junior year.

- ○ __ Consult with your son's high school coach and counselor before registering with the NCAA Eligibility Center. Why? There is a fee associated with registering with the NCAA Eligibility Center, and in most cases, it can be waived. However, you must go through your counselor to obtain such fee waiver.

- __ If your son hasn't received any college offers, continue with identifying 2-5 colleges to visit for Junior Days, unofficial visits, and camps he wants to attend during the summer before his senior year. (Visit each of the prospect colleges' websites to obtain dates of upcoming camps.)

- __ Create your upcoming summer calendar!
- __ Start saving money if you haven't already for the summer session.
- __ Continue with ACT Prep classes.
- __ Schedule your son to take the ACT.
- __ Ensure your son has a regular medical check-up. Stay on top of getting him medical treatment if he experiences any injuries, big or small.
- __ Review his progress reports to determine if you need to schedule a meeting with his teachers/counselors.
- __ Consider gifting your son's teachers with something thoughtful for Teacher Appreciation Day. This special day will normally fall on a Tuesday during the National Teacher Appreciation Week, which is the first full week of May.
- __ By the end of this year, your son should've taken at least 4-6 core courses:
    - __ 1 English class
    - __ 1 math class
    - __ 1 social studies class
    - __ 1 social science class
    - __ 1 comparative religion or foreign language class (This should be

the last religion and foreign language class he is required to take.)

SENIOR YEAR

Summer Before Senior Year

- __ Plan to attend any approved official visits that have been scheduled, as well as any camps. Again, if your son hasn't received any offers yet, attend any scheduled Junior Days on your list.
- __ Between May and June of this summer, consider allowing your son to pick one college offer from his Top College Choices list to commit to. (Ensure he has first had an official visit to the college he will be committing to.)
- __ If your son's final junior year report included a D or F in any class, enroll him in summer school to retake those classes, if available. If he doesn't have any D's or F's but he has over four C's in core classes, have him enroll in at least one summer core class to help push the C to a B. (Note: all core classes are locked in after this summer and cannot be retaken.) If your son has

all C's in his core classes he will yield a 2.0 core GPA.

- __ Continue with 7-on-7 team efforts if it's helping with his exposure and experience.
- __ Ensure your son has a regular medical check-up. Stay on top of getting him medical treatment if he experiences any injuries, big or small.

Senior Year

- __ Schedule a meeting with your son's new teachers.
- __ Schedule your son to retake the ACT, if needed.
- __ Consider gifting your son's teachers with something thoughtful for Teacher Appreciation Day. This special day will normally fall on a Tuesday during the National Teacher Appreciation Week, which is the first full week of May.
- __ Ensure your son has a regular medical check-up. Stay on top of getting him medical treatment if he experiences any injuries, big or small.
- __ By the end of this year, your son should've taken at least 4-6 core courses:

- ◦ __ 1 English class
- ◦ __ 1 math class
- ◦ __ 1 social studies class
- ◦ __ 1 social science class

After Graduation

- __ Prep for his college freshman year!

A FOOTBALL MOM'S PRAYER

God, my Father, I offer you my child.
You gave him to me, and he belongs to you
always.
Help me raise him in your ways. May I see him
the way You see him.
I ask You to guide him all the days of his life.
Lord, may he find his purpose in life and fulfill it.
Protect and cover him every time he touches that
field.
Keep his feet from stumbling.
Place him in the right places at the right times,
for the right opportunities.
Bless him with a spirit of discernment.
Help him make the right decisions.
Place the right people in his life and help him
identify the ones that do not belong.
Lord, help me fulfill the plan and purpose that
you have for me.

Remind me of who I am in You.

Give me the strength and joy I need on this earth.

Guide my thoughts and my heart.

May your love fulfill me and keep us safe from harm.

Amen.

ACKNOWLEDGEMENTS

This book couldn't have been possible without the support of my family, friends, and work associates. I am grateful for my friends and work associates for encouraging me to publish this book.

A special thank you to my mom, Alva Brule', and my grandmother, Alma Brule', for your unwavering love, support, and prayers!

Thank you to T. Hull, J. Juluke, J. Martin, A. Blanche for reading the raw manuscript and providing amazing feedback.

To my creative director, Trebreh, thank you times a million!

Job well done to my editor and partner, Nakia J.S. Thomas. I couldn't have done this without your help!

To my relatives, friends, and others who have

shared their support, either mentally, physically, spiritually, or financially, thank you!

ABOUT THE AUTHOR

Alvianne Brule' is a dynamic speaker, sports agent, mentor, philanthropist, entrepreneur, and athlete's advocate who is passionate about transforming athletes (as well as their families) into knowledgeable and successful superstars on and off the field. With nearly a decade of work behind the scenes of the sports industry, she has built a powerful platform and reputation known for relentlessly pushing the bounds in her field and creating monumental change for others. Alvianne Brule' is the CEO of The VIIITH full-service marketing and sports agency. She resides in New Orleans, LA, where she enjoys trying new foods and recipes and spending quality time with friends.

STAY CONNECTED with Alvianne by emailing her at info@dearfootballmoms.com or visiting alviannebrule.com. You can also find her on all social media platforms as @AlvianneBrule.

33280307R00091

Made in the USA
San Bernardino, CA
20 April 2019